GLOBETROTTER™

Travel Guide

MALTA

BRIAN RICHARDS

NEW HOLLAND

★★★ Highly recommended
★★ Recommended
★ See if you can

This edition first published in 2000
by New Holland Publishers (UK) Ltd
London • Cape Town • Sydney • Auckland
First edition published in 1996
10 9 8 7 6 5

24 Nutford Place
London W1H 6DQ
United Kingdom

80 McKenzie Street
Cape Town 8001
South Africa

14 Aquatic Drive
Frenchs Forest, NSW 2086
Australia

218 Lake Road
Northcote, Auckland
New Zealand

ISBN 1 85974 594 6

Commissioning Editor: Tim Jollands
Manager Globetrotter Maps: John Loubser
Editors: Thea Grobbelaar, Sara Harper, Donald Reid
Picture Researcher: Emily Hedges
Design and DTP: Lyndall Hamilton
Cartography: Éloïse Moss
Compiler/Verifier: Elaine Fick

Reproduction by Hirt & Carter (Pty) Ltd, Cape Town
Printed and bound in Hong Kong by Sing Cheong Printing Co. Ltd.

Dedication:
To my wife Sandra, as enthusiastic a visitor to Malta over the past 20 years as myself, and daughter Claire.

Acknowledgements:
The publishers and author gratefully acknowledge the generous assistance during the compilation of this book of Air Malta; Belleair Holidays; Corinthia Group of Companies; Malta Tourist Office, London; National Tourism Organisation of Malta; Suncrest Hotel, Qawra.

Photographic Credits:
John Johnston, page 110
Mary Evans Picture Library, pages 14, 15, 18, 19
Paul Murphy, pages 8, 10, 12, 16, 65 (top), 70, 82 (top), 83
Brian Richards, front cover, pages 7, 9, 11, 20, 23, 24, 25, 26, 27, 28, 29, 34, 35, 37, 38, 39, 40, 41, 42, 43, 45, 46, 48, 50, 56, 60, 61, 62, 63, 64, 65 (bottom), 66, 68, 76, 80 (bottom), 82 (bottom), 91, 92, 93, 94, 101, 106, 109, 111, 112, 113 top, 114 (top), 116, 117 (right), 118, 119, 120
Robert Harding Picture Library, title page, pages 4, 6, 13, 17, 22, 30, 33, 36, 44, 52, 54, 58, 71, 72, 74, 75, 78, 80 top, 84, 86, 88, 96, 99, 100, 102, 104, 108, 113 (bottom), 114 (bottom), 115, 117 left.

Cover: *Colourful Spinola Bay at St Julian's.*
Title page: *A Maltese woman in national dress, with one of the islands' lively* luzzu *fishing boats.*

CONTENTS

F126

1 Introducing Malta

Rugged limestone outcrops rising out of the glittering Mediterranean Sea, the Maltese islands are a compact and fascinating blend of history, holidays and friendly small-island hospitality. Malta's colourful past ranges from its earliest inhabitants, who built temples on the islands some 6500 years ago, to the arrival of crusading knights in the Middle Ages and the full brunt of World War II hostilities four centuries later. Added to the best climate in southern Europe, it helps attract more than a million tourists to the islands each year.

The islands are made for sightseeing. History beckons in every town and village, in the wealth of palaces, churches and fortifications that have survived down the centuries. High on every visitor's sightseeing list is the fortified capital **Valletta**. Rising in imposing grandeur from **Grand Harbour**, it is the focal point of urban Malta, which stretches from the resorts of **Sliema** and **St Julian's** to the historical **Three Cities**, and is home to 90% of the islands' population.

The ancient walled city of **Mdina** dominates the centre of the island, an area characterized by small towns and villages, each with its own impressive church. In the south are ancient temples and small fishing resorts, while to the north is the tourist development sprawled around **St Paul's Bay** and Malta's half-dozen or so sandy beaches.

Across the Comino Channel lies the smaller, greener island of **Gozo** and between them tiny **Comino**. Both are popular and attractive getaways for the holiday-maker.

Top Attractions

*** **Valletta:** centuries of history within the capital's high ramparts.
*** **Mdina:** medieval walled city of narrow streets and tight alleyways.
*** **Gozo:** spend at least a day investigating Malta's green sister isle.
** **Harbour cruise:** for unforgettable aspects of Valletta and the Three Cities.
** **St Julian's:** dine alfresco by the bay as the sun goes down and the nightlife starts.
* **Marsaxlokk:** fishing harbour packed with brightly painted *luzzu* boats.

Opposite: *Mġarr harbour in Gozo, a classic scene of harbour, historic fortifications and church spire.*

FACTS AND FIGURES

- The Maltese islands lie in the Mediterranean Sea 93km (58 miles) south of Sicily, 368km (230 miles) north of Tripoli and 288km (180 miles) east of Tunis.
- Malta measures 27km (17 miles) by 14.5km (9 miles), with an area of 246km^2 (95 sq miles).
- Gozo is 15km (9.5 miles) by 7km (4 miles) – an area of 67km^2 (26 sq miles). Comino is 2.7km^2 (1 sq mile).
- The shoreline of Malta is 137km (86 miles) long; Gozo's is 43km (27 miles).
- The highest point in the islands is 253m (829ft), southeast of Dingli village in Malta.
- The population of the islands is 350,000.

THE LAND

Malta is both the name of the nation and of the largest of the Maltese islands; Gozo is 8km (5 miles) to the northwest and midway between them is Comino. The island group, which also includes uninhabited Filfla and Cominotto, extends for 45km (28 miles) from northwest to southeast in the centre of the Mediterranean basin.

The islands offer contrasting scenery. Malta largely comprises a limestone plateau that slopes gently from high southern cliffs to the heavily indented northern coast. **Gozo** is blessed with an underlying layer of blue clay that helps to conserve precious rainwater and makes it more fertile. Tiny **Comino** is barren in the extreme.

There are no mountains or rivers in Malta. On higher ground, outcrops of hard coralline **limestone**, most of which has been eroded away, contribute towards the larger island's rugged and semi-arid appearance. Lower down, rough limestone walls bound small enclosures of reddish-brown soil which, despite the annual summer drought, yield a surprisingly wide variety of crops.

Cliffs rising above 250m (800ft) characterize Malta's southern shore – for most of its length there is no way down. Midway along the opposite coast are the impressive inlets of Grand Harbour, with its offshoot creeks, and Marsamxett Harbour. Between the built-up areas the shoreline is rocky. Malta's **beaches** are in the far north, where stretches of golden sand fill the bays either side of Marfa Ridge.

Gozo, a quarter Malta's size, has the same geological structure but varies in character. Flat-capped hills supporting many of the island's villages rise above the green valleys that separate them. This is the garden island, supplying the islands with much of their fruit and vegetable produce.

The Sea

Above: *Rugged limestone cliffs at Għar Hasan on the south coast.*

Opposite: *The expanse of Mellieħa Bay in the north.*

The sea around the Maltese islands is as clean and clear as anywhere in the Mediterranean. It is pleasant to bathe in, excellent for scuba diving and snorkelling and kindly accommodating to a wide array of water sports.

The best **dive sites** are off the steep southern cliffs of both Malta and Gozo, where underwater visibility is mostly between 6 and 20m (20 to 66ft), but can be 40m (132ft) or more. Diving is good year-round, with conditions exceptional between June and October when the sea's surface temperature tops 21°C (70°F).

Bathing off the rocky foreshore is generally safe – flags in the resorts warn of dangerous currents – and the warm water is sometimes at its best in the evening after the beaches have emptied. The smooth rock foreshore at Sliema is a popular spot for diving into the sea. Around the resorts there are plenty of places with boats, canoes and other water sports equipment for hire and sheltered bays in which to **sail**, **windsurf** and **waterski.** For those wishing to keep their feet dry, **boat trips** operate around the islands and to Comino's spectacular Blue Lagoon, where even the most committed landlubber will be tempted to take a dip. Other fascinating trips explore the subterranean world by glass-panelled underwater safari boat and submarine.

Malta puts its **seawater** to good practical use. Since the mid-1980s, it has established a series of reverse osmosis seawater conversion plants around its coastline; they now fulfil more than half the Maltese islands' freshwater needs and have cured the once-acute water shortage problems that dogged the country.

Where to Stay

A star grading system operates for hotels in Malta and Gozo, ranging from one to five stars; with few exceptions, tour operators feature hotels of three stars and above. Independent travellers should try to make their peak season reservations before arriving in the islands as hotels fill up quickly. There are also aparthotels, guesthouses and self-catering accommodation in holiday complexes and villas. Gozo's converted self-catering farmhouses, often with their own pool, are luxurious.

MALTA	J	F	M	A	M	J	J	A	S	O	N	D
AVERAGE TEMP. °C	13	13	14	16	19	25	26	26	24	20	18	14
AVERAGE TEMP. °F	55	55	57	61	66	78	79	79	76	69	64	58
Hours of Sun Daily	5	6	7	8	10	12	13	12	9	7	6	5
RAINFALL mm	83	55	40	22	10	2	0	0	30	83	87	97
RAINFALL in	3	2	2	1	0.5	0	0	0	1	3	3	4
Days of Rainfall	14	11	9	6	3	1	0	0	3	9	11	14
Sea Temp. °C	15	14	15	16	18	21	24	25	24	22	19	17
Sea Temp. °F	59	58	59	61	64	70	75	77	75	72	66	62

Climate

Malta's climate is just about the best the Mediterranean can offer – a hot summer sun blazes from a cloudless sky and the mild winter days have sufficient rain to green up the rocky landscape. The country's appeal as a year-round holiday destination owes much to the weather pattern. With one of Europe's best sunshine records, Malta is ideal both for a seaside 'burn' and a culturally motivated short break out of season.

In July and August the thermometer regularly hits the upper 30s Celsius (mid-90s Fahrenheit). The average for those months is a gloriously warm 26°C (79°F). Take care with sunbathing – remember that Malta is further south than parts of North Africa and that the sun deserves more respect than usual. Take sunglasses, too – the strong sun reflects off Malta's light-coloured buildings with real intensity. Overall the sunshine quota is generous, with a daily average of around 12 hours in high summer and even five hours a day in deepest winter.

Below: *Crowded beach umbrellas provide a colourful contrast to sand and sky at Golden Bay.*

While the wind blows mostly from the northwest (the wind is known as the *majjistral* in winter, when it blows strongest), the northeasterly *grigal* and northerly *tramuntana* can cause the odd storm from late summer onwards. Better known is the *sirocco* or *xlokk*, the warm and humid southeasterly wind that blows off the Sahara and can roughen up the sea along the southern shores. Malta's rainfall averages around 500mm (20in) annually, but can be half that figure in a drought year or double it if the winter months are particularly wet.

Flora and Fauna

Malta packs a surprising diversity of produce into the small fields packed between dry rubble walls that crisscross its countryside. Terraced cultivation of the hillsides and careful irrigation of low-lying arable land also help maximize the country's agricultural output. On Gozo, known as 'Malta's kitchen', the presence of water-retaining blue clay soil means the island remains greener than its larger sister and is thus able to provide much of the islands' food requirements.

Above: *A poppy field colours the countryside above Salina Bay.*

Crops reared in the thin soil covering include potatoes, tomatoes, onions, capers, wheat, maize, melons and sesame – plus animal fodder for winter. Small plantations of olives, figs, carobs, oranges and lemons exist, but grapes are the main fruit grown. These are mostly used to make the local wine. Fields are fallow in summer, when the sun parches all growth; by mid-autumn the ground is greener. Winter's vegetation is richer than you could ever imagine in high summer, while spring bursts forth in a bright array of roadside flowers and glorious fields of colour.

Wildlife in Malta and Gozo is scarce and restricted to lizards, geckos, the occasional snake and those birds, mostly migratory, fortunate enough not to have been trapped or blasted from the sky by hunters. The reservoirs of Chadwick Lakes near Rabat and the Għadira Nature Reserve at Mellieħa Bay are the only bird habitats, providing visiting ornithologists with a variety of sightings in spring and early autumn.

Wild flowers abound in autumn, winter and spring – more than 600 varieties that carpet the valleys, ravines and ridges of the Maltese islands with a blaze of colour. There are few **trees**, however. Most of the forest that once covered Malta was destroyed long ago to provide wood for ships and buildings and only the trees of Buskett Gardens survive.

Malta's Endangered Visitors

The Maltese islands' position midway between Europe and North Africa makes them a convenient touchdown point for birds which breed in northern Europe and winter further south. Some birds make Malta their winter home and in the process become even more dependent on the efforts of the Malta Ornithological Society to protect them from hunters. An estimated 25,000 hunters trap small songbirds and sell them in cages, and up to a million migratory birds are shot or trapped in large nets each year.

Above: *Symbol of an island republic: the familiar Maltese Cross was introduced by the knights in the mid-16th century.*

HISTORY IN BRIEF

Long before man arrived, the Maltese islands were joined to both Europe and Africa. The first inhabitants probably came about 7000 years ago from Sicily, which is only 93km (58 miles) away. These were early **Neolithic** people who farmed and reared animals, used stone implements, made pottery and eked out an existence in isolated communities.

Later generations were the builders of ancient temples and tombs cut from rock, awe-inspiring handiwork dating from before 2000BC which can still be seen throughout Malta and Gozo. Successive incursions of Bronze Age colonists followed before the arrival of **Phoenician** civilization in Malta around the 9th century BC.

The Phoenicians traded with the western Mediterranean and initially sought refuge in Malta's natural harbours. They brought prosperity to the islands, which subsequently came under the influence of their descendants, the **Carthaginians** – who, from their base in Tunis, gave Malta strategic importance for the first time. With Rome's influence in southern Italy growing, conflict between the **Romans** and Carthaginians was inevitable. In the firing line, Malta became a military base in the **First Punic War** (262–242BC), when it was sacked by the Romans. Though the Carthaginians regained control, Malta was seized again by the Romans in the **Second Punic War** (218BC) and stayed tied to Rome.

Malta prospered under Roman rule and important towns developed where Mdina and Victoria now stand. However, Malta retained many Phoenician influences and opinion is still divided over whether Malta's name originates in the Phoenician *malat*, meaning port, or the Roman *meli*, meaning honey. It was under the Romans that one of the most important happenings in Maltese history occurred – the shipwreck of St Paul the Apostle on Malta in AD60 and the conversion of the islands to Christianity.

The Maltese Cross

The eight-pointed cross – now known as the Maltese Cross because of its long association with the island – was introduced to Malta as the emblem of the **Knights of St John**. The eight points represent the eight Beatitudes; the four arms stand for the four virtues – prudence, temperance, fortitude and justice. It shouldn't be confused with the George Cross which appears on Malta's flag.

Historical Calendar

5000–3750BC Malta populated by Neolithic farmers from Sicily.
3750–2000BC Great period of temple building that includes Tarxien and Ġgantija.
800–218BC Malta under the Phoenicians and Carthaginians.
218BC Romans take Malta in second Punic War.
AD60 St Paul shipwrecked.
5th/6th centuries Roman power in decline; Byzantines rule Malta.
AD870 Arabs conquer Malta.
1090 Roger the Norman captures Malta from the Arabs.
1282 After periods of German and French domination, Malta comes under Aragon (Spain).
1530 The Knights of the Order of St John of Jerusalem arrive in Malta, a gift to the Order by Charles V of Spain.
1565 Great Siege of Malta.
1566 Valletta prepared as Knights' new capital.
1571 Valletta replaces Birgu as capital.
1798 Malta falls to the French under Napoleon. The Knights are ordered from the islands.
1800 The British move in; the French are evicted.
1814 Malta becomes a British Crown Colony.
1921 Self-government gives Malta responsibility for its own domestic affairs.
1940 First air raid on Malta in World War II.
1942 Malta is awarded the George Cross after 154 consecutive days of bombing.
1964 Malta independent.
1974 Malta becomes a republic within the Commonwealth.
1979 British forces leave Malta.
1998 Malta reaffirms bid to become a full member of the European Union.

With the decline of the Roman Empire in the fifth century, Malta found new masters in the **Byzantines**. In AD870 the **Arabs** conquered Malta from their base in Sicily and held the island for more than two centuries. Their influence still shows in the Maltese language spoken today and the many place names of Arab origin.

When Count Roger the Norman led an invasion from his kingdom in Sicily in 1090 and restored Christianity under **Norman** rule, the Arabs were allowed to remain for a while. As Sicily switched hands, so did Malta; western European influences increasingly prevailed and by 1282 Malta found itself administered by the **Spanish**.

In 1530, Holy Roman Emperor Charles V granted Malta to the **Knights of the Order of St John of Jerusalem**; their stay as masters of Malta lasted until the 1798 capitulation to Napoleon's **French** forces.

Maltese life under the French was brief. In 1800 the **British** assumed control and the 1814 Treaty of Paris confirmed Malta's status under the British crown for 150 years until the granting of independence in 1964. The Maltese islands, once more of high strategic importance, played a heroic role during World War II in the face of incredible odds which earned them the George Cross. In 1974 Malta became a republic within the Commonwealth.

Above: *Malta's national flag since the country became independent from Great Britain in 1964.*

Galleys of the Knights

The galleys that carried the Knights into battle were in the style of the Greek and Roman galleys. A typical galley 55m (180ft) long and 6m (20ft) wide would have a draught of just 2.3m (7½ft) – ideal for calm summer conditions but little good in winter, when the vessels would be laid up in Dockyard Creek off Grand Harbour. It took some 240 slaves seated six to a cross-bench to propel the galley at a speed of only two knots; in battle it would have been defended by a bow cannon and other light arms.

Below: *Philippe Villiers de l'Isle Adam, the first Grand Master on Malta.*

The Knights of St John

In 1530 Malta was given by **Charles V**, Holy Roman Emperor and King of Spain and Sicily, to the Knights of the Order of St John of Jerusalem. This powerful chivalric Order had been founded 400 years earlier as the Frères Hospitaliers de St Jean de Jerusalem, a group of monks attached to a hospital which had been set up for pilgrims in Jerusalem.

Their hospitality included providing escorts through the Levant; they became armed and gradually military duties took over. After the successful First Crusade, which ended in 1099, the Knights became a full military order, but still combining soldiering with nursing. Nearly 200 years later, the Order was turned out of the Holy Land by the Moslems and sought refuge in **Cyprus**.

In 1310 the Order left Cyprus for **Rhodes**. Over the next two centuries the Knights of Rhodes, as they were now known, became wealthier and ever more powerful, and built up a navy to defend their shores. It was not powerful enough, though, to overcome the 400-strong Turkish fleet of Suleiman the Magnificent in 1522 and after a six-month siege the Knights were sent packing once more.

For seven difficult years under Grand Master **Philippe Villiers de l'Isle Adam** they sought a new base. A temporary home was secured in Italy and France before the offer of Malta, first made in 1523, was unenthusiastically accepted. The Order was given the Maltese islands, together with Tripoli, in perpetuity for an annual rent of a falcon. After the ideal conditions of Rhodes, Malta was viewed in a poor light. The Knights found it infertile, unfortified and with too few inhabitants to mount a presentable defensive force.

Above: *One of two bronze cannon guarding the cathedral in Mdina.*

Early Days in Malta

While the Knights were unsure about Malta, the Maltese received their new tightly disciplined masters with caution; it took a common enemy, the **Turks**, to bring about full conciliation. On arrival in Malta, the Knights found the main settlements to be the fortified city of **Mdina** and the village of **Birgu** by Grand Harbour – they chose Birgu (now Vittoriosa) as their base because it offered mooring for their oared galleys off Grand Harbour. The Grand Master set himself up in Fort St Angelo at the end of the Birgu peninsula.

Vows of the Knights

The Knights, committed to defence of the Church and care of the sick, maintained a secular lifestyle through vows of chastity, obedience and poverty. Additionally, they pledged never to fight against another Christian country, never to gamble or run into debt and never to shrink from battle.

To join the Order, a prospective Knight of Justice had to be Catholic, of aristocratic birth and able to provide a dowry – once accepted, he was established for life. Other grades of membership in the Order were Chaplain and serving brothers; two honorary grades, Magistral Knight and Knight of Grace, were bestowed on those who had given outstanding service. When a Knight died, the Order inherited his estate.

The Eight Langues

The Knights were split into nationalities, or *langues*, as a measure of convenience in battle. There were eight langues, although those of **Auvergne**, **France** and **Provence** would nowadays be regarded as one. Other langues were **Aragon**, **Castile**, **England**, **Germany** and **Italy**; the English langue lapsed with the Reformation led by King Henry VIII in 1540.

Each langue was headquartered in an *auberge*, a hostel with its own accommodation, dining hall (where the

The Greatest Leader

No Grand Master made a greater impact as head of the Order than Frenchman **Jean Parisot de la Valette**. Born in 1494, he joined the Order aged 20 and became Grand Master in 1557, 27 years after the Knights' arrival in Malta. His first task as head of the Order was to strengthen Malta's defences in anticipation of a Turkish invasion; his greatest hour came with the capitulation of the Turks that ended the Great Siege of 1565. La Valette gave his name to the new fortified capital on Mount Sciberras, inaugurated on 28 March 1566; he died in 1568 and is buried in St John's Co-Cathedral in Valletta.

Above: *The raising of the Great Siege in 1565.* **Opposite:** *A depiction of the Turkish invasion.*

food was reputed to be excellent) and chapel. At first these were in Birgu; when Valletta became the capital, the langues moved to larger premises there. At the head of the Order was the **Grand Master**, responsible only to the Pope and elected for life. In all, 28 Grand Masters presided over the Knights in Malta between 1530 and 1798; the longest-serving was **Manuel Pinto de Fonseca** (1741–73), founder of the university.

By the time the Knights had come through the Great Siege of 1565 and made their base in the new capital of Valletta six years later, the Order was being overtaken by progress. The Knights had long ago found ways round their poverty vows and had assembled a fleet of sailing ships to replace their galleys, but these would prove insufficient to take on the sea might of the Mediterranean powers.

In 1798, **Napoleon** ended the Knights' presence on Malta without a shot being fired. The French fleet stopped by on its way to Egypt and issued an ultimatum to the Knights' first German Grand Master, **Ferdinand de Hompesch**. The Order hastily surrendered Malta to the French and within three days had left the island with only their personal belongings, never to return.

The Great Siege

The Knights' reputation as defenders of Christendom and the Maltese islands peaked in a bloody four-month battle with the **Turks** in 1565. It came to be known as the Great Siege, in which 700 Knights and 9000 Maltese held out against Turkey's military might of 30,000 men and an armada of 200 ships sent by the Sultan, **Suleiman the Magnificent**.

The Turks were feared throughout the eastern Mediterranean as aggressors and conquerors, but saw Malta under the Knights as an ever-present threat to their quest for territorial gains in southern Europe. To this end, Gozo was sacked in 1551 and some 6000

Barbarity in War

The fall of Fort St Elmo to the Turks on 23 June 1565 after 31 days of unbroken siege precipitated savagery unmatched at any stage in the battle. The Turkish commander Mustapha Pasha, having lost 8000 men in taking the fort, ordered the decapitation of several important Knights; the heads were impaled on stakes facing Fort St Angelo and the torsos, nailed to planks, were set adrift in Grand Harbour. Four bodies reached the opposite shore, prompting immediate retaliation from Grand Master La Valette. He ordered the execution of all the Turkish prisoners in Fort St Angelo, loaded the severed heads into cannon and fired them back across Grand Harbour at the Turks in Fort St Elmo.

inhabitants – almost the entire population – reduced to slavery. Encouraged by this success, the Turks laid plans for a large-scale attack on Malta. It was known by the autumn of 1564 that an invasion was inevitable and in preparation the Knights under Grand Master **Jean Parisot de la Valette** had strengthened Fort St Elmo and Fort St Angelo which guarded Grand Harbour. La Valette's request for European help had been ignored and the Turkish fleet arrived off Malta on 18 May 1565.

The Attack on St Elmo

Target of the Turks' initial assault was Fort St Elmo, which held out for 31 days against repeated attacks before capitulating. The Turks lost 8000 men, including their leader **Dragut Rais**; some 1500 defenders, including 130 Knights, were killed.

Next the Turks turned on Birgu and Senglea, which had been strengthened by limited reinforcements from Sicily. A great chain slung across the dividing creek kept

DRESSED TO KILL

After three months of siege action around Grand Harbour in the summer of 1565, the Turkish commander-in-chief Mustapha Pasha turned his attentions to Mdina. The fortified capital on its rocky bluff could only be taken from the south and with an attack imminent, Mdina's Governor Don Mesquita dreamed up a bold plan to frighten off the invaders. With only a small garrison, he had the peasants and their womenfolk dress in soldiers' uniforms and parade with the troops along the ramparts. The ploy worked. Faced by what they thought was a mighty well-armed garrison, the Turks retreated and Mdina was spared.

BEST OF BRITISH

Around Malta you will see everywhere evidence of 179 years of British presence:
- Above every police station door is the classic British police force blue lamp.
- Older telephone boxes and letter boxes are red.
- Most of Malta's old cars – the Ford Anglias, Vauxhall Victors and Morris Minors – were made in Britain.
- Vintage buses also carry the painted names of manufacturers such as Leyland, Bedford and AEC, although their true British pedigree is more doubtful.
- Driving, as in Britain, is on the left, and as you do you may find yourself travelling past such establishments as Coronation Store and the Britannia Bar.

the invading fleet at bay while defenders in the two positions repulsed a barrage of enemy attacks – again with huge loss of Turkish life.

The assault lasted several weeks, but with morale declining in the oppressive heat and disease further decimating their forces, the Turks finally fled for home. Two-thirds of the invasion force had been killed in the conflict between Christian and Muslim.

The French and the British

French control over the Maltese islands was brief but destructive. After the Knights had been sent packing in 1798, Napoleon did away with the privilege of nobility; his forces plundered any spoils left by the Knights and defaced many of the Order's buildings. All manner of restrictions were placed upon the Catholic Church and its property continued to be plundered.

This led to a **revolt** by the Maltese in Mdina which spread rapidly throughout the island. The French complement of 4000 men retreated to the towns around Grand Harbour and stayed there until a **British** blockade under Captain Alexander Ball, aided by the Maltese, forced their surrender in September 1800.

Malta was at first seen by the British as having bargaining value rather than the strategic worth that had been so readily recognized by Napoleon. But the Maltese took to their new masters and, anticipating a return of the exiled Knights under Russian or Neapolitan protection, argued strongly that the islands should become a British colony.

The relationship confirmed by the **Treaty of Paris** in 1814 was to last for 164 years. Malta's value to Britain as a

Below: *A blue lamp in evidence at St Paul's Bay police station.*

naval base increased throughout the 19th century, aiding territorial expansion further east and the Crimean War effort. The opening of the **Suez Canal** in 1869, combined with the development of steamships, gave Malta and Aden dual prominence as coaling stations on the sea route to the Far East.

By the turn of the century, trade growth resulting from the steamship era had left Malta trailing rival Mediterranean ports. Dockyard employment increased during **World War I**, when Malta again played the role of 'nurse of the Mediterranean'; during the conflict, while Maltese signed up with British service units, the islands provided 25,000 beds for the wounded and sick.

In 1921, Malta became self-governing in local matters, leaving Britain to take care of wider issues like foreign policy. But the system failed and in 1930 the constitution was suspended – to be restored two years later and again suspended in 1933. It took the onset of World War II (*see* p. 18) to unite the dissident factions.

After the war Malta received £30 million from the British government to help rebuild the island and in 1947 self-government was re-established. The mid-1950s saw an imaginative plan to fully integrate Malta with Britain, with Maltese MPs to be returned to Westminster. The plan was however rejected in a referendum as the Maltese Church was not keen to join with the Anglican.

On 21 September 1964, Malta achieved **independence**, but chose to maintain ties with Britain. The Queen remained sovereign of the islands and Malta stayed within the Commonwealth. Under the Nationalist government, British forces were to remain in Malta for 10 years in return for £50 million in grants; when **Dom Mintoff**'s Labour party took office in 1971 this was renegotiated and the last British forces in Malta sailed out of Grand Harbour on 31 March 1979. Malta became a republic within the Commonwealth in 1974, the Queen's place as head of state going to a Maltese President, appointed for five years by the House of Representatives.

Victoria Lines

A series of fortifications running the length of the high ridge just north of Mosta, built by the British between 1875 and 1885, took the name Victoria Lines in 1897 to mark the diamond jubilee of Queen Victoria. The forts and gun-batteries include Fort Bingemma in the west, Fort Mosta and Targa Battery in the centre and Fort Madliena in the east, all linked by a masonry parapet. By the turn of the century their military value was in question and in 1907 the Victoria Lines were abandoned. With EU funding, they are being renovated as a tourist attraction.

Below: *A panel on the Palace of the Grand Masters in Valletta commemorating the award of the George Cross in 1942.*

Safe from the Bombs

The Maltese minimized loss of life during World War II by constructing air-raid shelters and relocating large numbers of the population from the Valletta and Grand Harbour area to safer parts of the island. The old railway tunnel between Valletta and Floriana provided a sanctuary for many during the bombing raids and, as in medieval times, people sought shelter in Mdina. Some 35,000 buildings throughout the islands suffered damage or were destroyed during the war – 11,000 of them in April 1942, the worst month of the bombing.

Malta in World War II

At the outbreak of World War II, Malta was Britain's most important Mediterranean naval base. As such, it was to protect west–east supply lines while blocking the passage between Italy and North Africa. When Mussolini plunged Italy into the war on 10 June 1940, Malta knew for sure that it was destined to play a frontline role. Europe was nine months into the conflict when, on 11 June, Malta suffered its first **air** attack on the dockyard.

At that point, Malta's entire anti-aircraft resources totalled 42 guns, two dozen searchlights and three Gloster Gladiator biplanes which had been discovered in crates and were hurriedly assembled. The Gladiators, christened *Faith*, *Hope* and *Charity*, were matched against 200 Italian aircraft based 100km (60 miles) north in Sicily. On the face of it there was surely no contest, but by forcing enemy aircraft to bomb from a greater height, the three small Glosters more than earned their keep. The Maltese people no longer felt like a sitting target, and for three long weeks the proud Gladiators defended Malta's air space alone until Hurricane support arrived.

In December 1940, the German air force moved into Sicily to support the Italians and with 250 aircraft the combined Axis forces outnumbered Malta's aerial strike force by four to one. Meanwhile, German and Italian **submarines** maintained a relentless assault on the supply convoys.

Below and opposite: *Italian publications record wartime air raids on Malta.*

Malta's Darkest Hour

Malta's worst period of the war was in early 1942, when the air raids never ceased. In April alone, 6700 tons of bombs rained down on the island and on the 15th of that month a special message from the British king, George VI, informed the people of Malta that they had collectively been awarded the **George Cross** for their unyielding bravery. Some relief was forthcoming with a delivery of Spitfires and slowly Maltese air power was built up to 200 aircraft. With a more powerful air combat force, Malta's position strengthened during 1942 and by October of that year, when the British Eighth Army succeeded at **El Alamein**, the Axis threat had been considerably weakened.

Targeting the Convoys

Ultimate control of the central Mediterranean hinged on supply lines and in the early months of 1942 the Allies suffered heavy shipping losses in the Malta-bound convoys. For much of the year the country's civil and military population was reduced to near starvation levels, relying on a communal feeding service and being forced to eat their diminishing animal stocks – not until early in 1943 did the rationing situation improve.

Cost of Malta's War

It took the Allied assault on Sicily in 1943 to effectively end Malta's close involvement in the war. The island acted as a fighter base during the operation to capture Sicily's airfields and once this had been achieved the Axis powers were unable to continue their harassment of shipping in the central Mediterranean. For Malta, three years of war had been intense. The islands had endured some of the most ruthless bombing of World War II and it was primarily because the buildings were of stone that huge sections of the towns were not destroyed by fire. Nearly 1500 Maltese civilians were killed in the air raids.

The clearing-up operation lasted for years. Valletta's bombed seaboard was still rubble into the 1950s and the rebuilding of the towns around Grand Harbour, now collectively known as the Three Cities, took nearly a decade.

THE SANTA MARIA CONVOY

In the summer of 1942, Malta was in dire need of food and fuel to continue its struggle against the Axis powers. As the Maltese prayed to Santa Maria, whose feast day was due on 15 August, Britain sent a convoy of 14 merchant ships under armed escort. As the ships neared Malta they came under massive air and sea attack. Nine merchantmen were sunk; the five remaining included the tanker *Ohio*, with 11,000 tons of fuel critical to Malta's survival. On 13 August four vessels limped into Grand Harbour. More prayers were offered to Santa Maria and on the morning of the 15th the *Ohio* reached Malta. The islands were saved and the name of the Santa Maria Convoy became legendary.

Dom Mintoff

The Maltese either loved or hated Dom Mintoff, the former Labour leader and Malta's best-known politician. The Oxford-educated civil engineer and architect served as Prime Minister from 1955–58 and 1971–84; throughout the 1970s his name was synonymous with that of Malta as he maintained non-alignment with the superpowers and distanced himself from the Catholic Church. Mintoff set himself apart on the world stage by demanding commercial aid from various left-wing leaders in preparation for the British military withdrawal in 1979.

GOVERNMENT AND ECONOMY

When independent Malta became a republic on 13 December 1974, economic stability was the priority facing the Labour government of Prime Minister **Dom Mintoff**. Ties with Britain were to be finally severed in March 1979 with the departure of British forces, leaving Malta to seek economic assistance elsewhere.

The British military withdrawal, at the end of an extended defence agreement made at independence in 1964, had a drastic effect on employment in the islands. The job losses were partly offset by widespread **emigration** to Canada and Australia; today as many Maltese live abroad, particularly in Australia, as in the islands themselves.

New Friends for Old

In the mid-1970s, Mintoff declared a policy of strict neutrality, cultivating closer friendships outside Europe with the likes of Russia, China and Libya that gave rise to unease in Europe. But the fears born out of Mintoff's worldly fraternizations proved without foundation – the previous Nationalist government had already pledged its future to Europe through an EEC association agreement, forerunner to Malta's application for full **European Union** membership on 16 July 1990.

Below: *A harbour cruise in Dockyard Creek: tourism now provides Malta with almost a third of its gross national product.*

Head-to-head Politics

Participation in Malta's two-party politics is a national pastime. Clubs for **Nationalist** and **Labour** followers proliferate, an indication of the close inter-party rivalry. In each intensely contested general election, the margin of victory is slender.

After three consecutive spells in government, the Labour party found itself shunted out by the Nationalists in 1987. **Dr Carmelo Mifsud Bonnici**, having replaced the retiring Mintoff as Prime Minister in 1984, was forced out of his Castile office three years later, when **Dr Eddie Fenech-Adami** took over the reins in the House of Representatives. Under the Nationalists, who were re-elected in 1992, and again in 1998 after a brief intervening Labour period, Malta has taken a firm pro-Europe stance, feeling that full EU membership will further strengthen its policy of non-alignment.

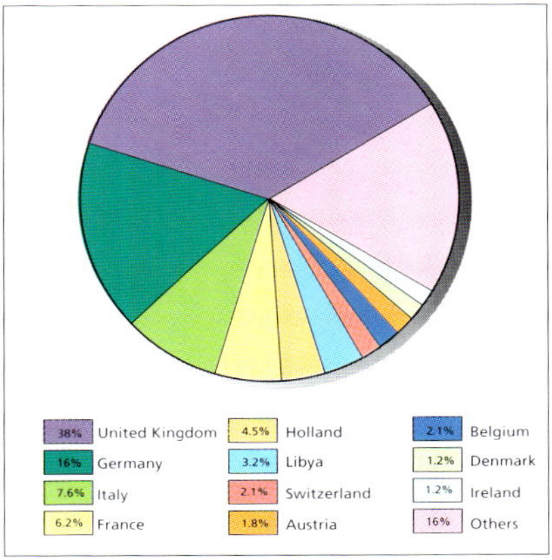

TOURIST ARRIVALS BY NATIONALITY

Tourism to the Fore

While other Mediterranean holiday destinations have seen their fortunes ebb and flow, Malta's popularity appears to know no bounds. Each year sees an increase in tourist numbers, with an all-time high of more than 1.2 million in 1999. The **British** love affair with Malta continues more than two decades into independence, with around 450,000 visitors from the United Kingdom annually.

Tourism is now Malta's principal industry, providing 24% of the country's gross national product. The highly impressive **Malta International Airport** terminal, able to handle 2.5 million departing passengers a year, was opened in 1992; two years later the new **cruise ship terminal** below Valletta's bastions received the first of many white-hulled cruise liners.

Shipshape Economy

Shipping continues to play a significant part in the economy, with Malta's dockyards successfully tendering for servicing and repair work on tankers and container ships plying the Mediterranean. Additionally, the Malta **Freeport** distribution centre in the south of the island has developed as a good foreign exchange earner. **Agriculture** also makes a solid contribution, despite the compact nature of Malta and Gozo.

Radio and TV

For such a small population, the Maltese people enjoy a vast selection of radio and TV – at the last count, 13 radio stations and 20 or so TV channels, plus 40-odd cable TV channels. Since the airways were opened to all in the early 1990s, the number of Maltese radio stations has grown to 11, plus the BBC World Service and Voice of the Mediterranean. While TV Malta remains the country's prime TV station, Maltese viewers also receive many Italian channels – the high-masted TV aerials you see on your travels around the island are needed for tuning in to Italy.

Above: *There's always time for a chat: men catch up on the local gossip in Republic Street, Valletta.*

THE PEOPLE

To the visitor, the locals might all be Maltese, but those born and bred in Gozo will claim they are Gozitan first, Maltese second. There has always been friendly rivalry between the two sets of islanders, with Malta people telling jokes about the 'mean' Gozitans and Gozo folk forever claiming intellectual superiority.

Down the centuries, despite domination by a succession of expansionist-minded invaders, the Maltese have clung steadfastly to their strong insular identity. Gregarious by nature among themselves, they are generally friendly towards visitors, though it will be noticed that waiters and others in the service industry often make little effort to please.

Typically among Latin races, the Maltese are devoted to the **family** and family life. Families are often large and stay closely in touch; in such a small island community parents, brothers, sisters, aunts, uncles and their various offspring all live within a short distance of each other.

As business in Malta tends to be male dominated, women are left to play the traditional home-caring role. It is today's generation of daughters, keen to develop their own careers, who are freeing themselves from the constraints of the past.

Attitudes to **dress** are conventional in Malta, a country of firm social traditions. Visitors should be suitably attired when entering churches to save causing offence. Topless sunbathing is against the law.

Close Families

It is said that a dozen Maltese family names are shared by 90% of the population; after a short time in Malta you will be familiar with most of them. Among the most popular surnames are Azzopardi, Borg, Calleja, Camilleri, Caruana, Galea, Gatt, Grech, Pace, Tabona, Vella and Zammit. Maltese families remain close-knit, continuing to live in the same town or village or often the same street. Don't be surprised to see a family gathering of 30 or more enjoying Sunday lunch together in a restaurant.

Religion

Malta's Roman Catholic roots run deep. The majority of the population is devoutly Catholic and the Church plays a large part in their lives, as is shown by the size of the churches in even the smallest villages. The islands have more than 350 churches, from the awesome edifices of St John's Co-Cathedral in Valletta and Xewkija's parish church on Gozo, down to those the size of the tiny chapel on Comino.

With four out of five Maltese regularly attending mass, the need for so many churches is readily apparent. Not all are in permanent use, however – some isolated chapels are unlocked only on feast days. Nearly all services are held in Malti.

Throughout the islands, **Holy Week** has special meaning. Large crowds turn out in towns and villages for the Good Friday processions – those in Rabat, Mosta, Qormi and Żebbuġ are among the largest. Local organizations march slowly at the head of the procession, focal point of which are the life-sized statues depicting the Passion and death of Christ, supported shoulder high by men in hooded white robes. The processions can last for hours and it takes six strong men to carry each of the painted wooden statues, with frequent pauses to rest. People dressed as soldiers and Biblical characters also march to the sombre music. The Easter Sunday procession, by contrast, is more of a parade. Usually led by the local band, it is a much happier occasion, with a statue of the risen Christ carried through the streets to the sound of church bells.

A traditional feature of **Christmas** is the illuminated crib displays, some with moving figures, to be found in several of Malta's village churches.

Sacred Spots

Malta's religious character shows in the number of shrines dotted about the islands – by the wayside and on street corners; even set in the wall of Valletta's ruined Opera House. Flickering candles in their red see-through holders and fresh flowers are an ever-present reminder of the Maltese people's strong religious convictions. Builders of Malta's old buses often incorporated a small, illuminated shrine behind the driver; some bone-shaking vehicles prominently spread the word that 'Jesus Lives'.

Craftware

The variety of traditional crafts still practised in Malta and Gozo come packaged in two craft villages – the former airfield site of **Ta' Qali** in Malta and **Ta' Dbiegi** in Gozo. Here you can watch skilled craftsmen in action and buy gold and silver filigree, decorative coloured glassware, ceramics, pottery, Malta stone ornaments in calcite onyx or limestone, wrought ironwork, brass door knockers and wicker furniture. Prices in the craft villages are competitive.

Below: *Colourful Maltese craftware for sale at the market place.*

MALTESE DRIVERS

Driving in Malta is on the left. Many Maltese, however, prefer the middle of the road (it's the shortest route and avoids the bumps) and the popular 1980s song *Maltese Calypso* made the now famous reference to the Maltese 'driving in the shade'. Local driving habits are unpredictable (to say the least) and call for vigilance, but pottering sedately around the roads of Malta and Gozo in the company of 170,000 other vehicles beats motorway driving any day.

In recent years the car hire scene has been transformed – up-to-date models with fitted seatbelts are now the rule and prices are among the best in Europe. Vehicle testing is soon to be introduced – a move that could see the end of the Morris Minors, Ford Prefects and Vauxhall Victors that are taken for their weekly spin round the island on Sunday afternoons.

Specialist **Gozitian** craftwork includes lace napkins, handkerchiefs and tablecloths, and cheap and chunky woollen jumpers and cardigans. Village women sit outside their homes in the cool of a summer's evening, chatting and working away with knitting needles or lace-maker's cushion. Durable hand-woven Malta Weave rugs, tablecloths, bedspreads and soft toys are other good buys.

Watercolours by local artists are also excellent value. Among the most popular artists is **Edwin Galea**, painter both of tranquil island landscapes and all-action sea battles depicting Maltese history from the Great Siege to the present day.

Language

Such is the Maltese familiarity with English that visitors need concern themselves only with the pronunciation of place names. Determined linguists will discover that the Maltese language of Malti, Phoenician-based with Arab modifications and later English and Italian influences, is complex and not the easiest to speak or understand.

The Village Festa

To the uninitiated, staccato crackling in the air above and accompanying bursts of thick smoke might imply that one Maltese village has declared war on another. To

Right: *Banners decorate the streets of towns and villages at festa time.*
Opposite: *A statue of the risen Christ is paraded through St Julian's on Easter Sunday.*

everyone else, the aerial explosions mean that another *festa* (festival) is under way. This is the highlight of every parish calendar, a five-day celebration of its patron saint's feast day wrapped round a weekend of non-stop action that successfully blends piousness with wild celebration. The festa season kicks off on the third Sunday after Easter with the Feast of **St Publius** in Floriana, and continues through to **September**. Colourful flags and bunting flap in the breeze and statues line the streets during festa week. The parish church is dressed, ornamented and lit up by hundreds of light bulbs for the occasion; inside the saint's statue is adorned with flowers. After the services, crowds follow the statue through the streets. A brass band plays and there is general merrymaking late into the night, culminating in a spectacular firework display which the villagers have saved for all year.

Place Names

Pronunciation difficulties are caused by accented letters (ċ = *ch*; ġ = *j*; ż = *ts*) and silent letters (għ; h, though aspirated at the end of a word; and q). Other pronunciations are: ħ = *h*; j = y; x = *sh*; m = *im* when an initial letter and followed by a consonant, as in Mdina. You may find yourself having to pronounce the following:

Dwejra (*d'way-rah*)
Ġgantija (*jee-gann-tee-yah*)
Għar Lapsi (*ahr-lapp-see*)
Għar Dalam (*ahr-dall-am*)
Għarb (*ahrb*)
Għasri (*ahs-ree*)
Haġar Qim (*ha-jah-eem*)
Lija (*lee-yah*)
Luqa (*loo-ah*)
Marsaxlokk (*mar-sah-shlok*)
Mdina (*im-deen-ah*)
Mġarr (*im-jarr*)
Mnajdra (*im-na-eed-ra*)
Mqabba (*im-ab-ba*)
Msida (*im-see-dah*)
Naxxar (*nash-shar*)
Qala (*ahl-ah*)
Qawra (*ow-rah*)
Qormi (*orr-me*)
Qrendi (*ren-dee*)
Siġġiewi (*sij-jee-e-wee*)
Ta' Ċenċ (*ta chench*)
Tarxien (*tar-she-en*)
Xagħra (*shuh-ra*)
Xewkija (*show-kee-yah*)
Xlendi (*shlen-dee*)
Żebbuġ (*zeb-booj*)

Festivals For All

- In July and August, the month-long **Maltafest** features local and foreign artists in concerts, recitals, open-air theatre, ballet and jazz performances.
- The **Malta Jazz Festival** takes place in Valletta over the last weekend in July and has a reputation for attracting star names.
- At around the same time the **Beer and International Food Festival** takes place at Ta' Xbiex.
- In early October, the **Birgu Festival** in Vittoriosa combines Maltese art, crafts and folklore with pageantry and re-enactments – the similarly-styled **Mdina Pageant** is held in Mdina in June.
- In November, the **International Choir Festival** attracts choirs from throughout Europe.

The Malta Experience

An established and popular screen attraction brings history to life at the Mediterranean Conference Centre, where Malta's fascinating story from Neolithic times to the present is told in an ever-changing kaleidoscope of images – 1100 colour slides from 21 projectors with sound effects, accompanied by multi-lingual commentary. Presentations of The Malta Experience take place hourly from 11:00–16:00 from Monday to Friday; from 11:00–13:00 at weekends and holidays.

After a period in the 1970s and 1980s when it was held in May, **Carnival** in Malta is now firmly established in the period immediately preceding Lent, to herald the approaching end of winter and arrival of spring. Carnival was started by the Knights in the 16th century, when it was led by the Grand Master; now towns and villages throughout Malta join in the celebrations with fancy-dress parades, lavishly decorated floats, folk dancing and, of course, firework displays. The biggest and most colourful procession takes place through the streets of Valletta.

Entertainment

Malta may not be renowned for its dynamic nightlife, but what there is caters adequately for a wide cross-section of holiday-makers and includes a **theatre**, **casino**, **cinemas** and **discos**. Most hotels offer entertainment of some kind, such as sing-along **piano bar**, **cabaret** or colourful **folk-dancing show**.

If it's loud **music** you're after, head for the neon-adorned music bars of Paceville and St George's Bay, thundering out their wild range of dance, house, rap and reggae offerings. There are some good hi-tech discos with wall-to-wall lasers and advanced sound systems to satisfy the most sophisticated boppers. It was not always thus – as recently as the 1980s, Paceville was still primarily residential, enlivened by just a scattering of restaurants.

Film buffs have been spoilt for choice since the expansion of the Eden Film Centre at St George's Bay to 16 screens, showing an interesting blend of brand new releases and older films – all in English. Other multi-screen cinema complexes have sprung up elsewhere in the island. Be prepared for incessant chatter and popcorn crunching during the film; also for the sudden picture fade-out and interval.

Below: *A summer evening's* bocci *game at Buġibba. Towns and villages throughout Malta have their own* bocci *clubs.*

The **Manoel Theatre** in Valletta, Malta's cultural hub, stages ballet, opera and concerts by its own symphony orchestra. Plays are performed, but rarely in English. The centre pages of the free *Welcome Holiday Guide* has a monthly update of performances, events, exhibitions and feast days.

Malta's Best Beaches

- **Mellieħa Bay** is Malta's longest beach, excellent for water sports, safe swimming and sunbathing.
- **Golden Bay** lives up to its name, with fine yellow sand and a range of water sports.
- **Għajn Tuffieħa Bay**, next to Golden Bay, is quiet without being secluded and is excellent for bathing.
- **Ġnejna Bay** is popular with the locals – a small beach with limited facilities but offering peace and quiet.
- **Ramla Bay** is Gozo's main beach, its soft yellow sand packed with sunbathers all through summer.
- **San Blas Bay** is Gozo's best-kept secret – a tiny beach at the foot of a steep path and strong on solitude.

Sport and Recreation

Malta's menfolk (but very few women) turn out in force on Sunday afternoons for the **trotting** meetings at Marsa, to enjoy the programme of a dozen or so races that takes nearly five hours to complete. Bet on the Tote (minimum 50c forecast; Lm1 win or place) and then sit in the sun and count your winnings. Admire the grace of movement as up to a dozen impeccably groomed beasts pace twice round the 1000m (⅔ mile) Marsa Race Track; the circuit has been there since 1868. Immediately outside the arena some of the 700 trotters registered with the Malta Racing Club are stabled. Trotting is Malta's most popular spectator sport and regularly attract crowds of up to 4000.

There are plenty of participant sports to occupy the visitor, from **golf** at the par-68, 5091m (5567yd) Royal Malta Golf Club to the **Malta Marathon**, held each February, and **tenpin bowling** at the computerized Eden Super Bowl in St George's Bay. The extensive Marsa Sports Club complex offers weekly or daily membership to visitors and includes **tennis**, **squash**, **mini-golf**, **billiards** and **swimming** in a freshwater pool. Increasingly, tennis and squash courts are found in hotels, as are **fitness centres**. The informal game of *bocci* – like the French boules but using a combination of balls and coloured wooden blocks – is a national pastime. Soccer is popular in Malta and top foreign teams have a strong following.

Below: *Trotting meeting at the Marsa Race Track.*

Malta and Gozo are renowned for their **water sports**. There are half a dozen diving schools in the islands and plenty of opportunities for sailing, waterskiing and windsurfing. Maltese teams do well at water polo, which is also a popular spectator sport. **Fishing** is possible either off the rocky foreshore or by arrangement with a local boatman; there are no organized excursions.

Above: *A selection of home-grown Maltese fare.*
Opposite: *Some of the wines now being produced on Gozo.*

Food and Drink

Consider the many foreign influences that have shaped Malta's character and it follows that the country's cuisine will be broad based – vaguely **Mediterranean**, flavoured with **Italian** and a dash of the **British**; possibly with a hint of **Arabian**. Many restaurants steer a culinary course between British and Italian, to satisfy the conservative palates of holiday-makers.

While genuine Maltese dishes appear on wider menus, there are still few restaurants specializing in the traditional cuisine of the islands. Nevertheless, there are many restaurants providing excellent fare, often in a rustic Maltese setting – though it is not necessarily the best for those thinking about their diet. Don't be put off by the sun-faded pictures of food outside.

Locally grown **vegetables** such as green peppers, globe artichokes, aubergines and marrows play a big part in Maltese cuisine. They can be stuffed with anchovies, minced pork or cheese to make a filling meal, possibly accompanied by thick chunks of Malta's excellent crusty **bread**.

Fast food and medium-fast food have long been established in Malta. There are dozens of **pizzerias**

Maltese Seafood

The Maltese serve fish in many ways – fried, grilled, poached, baked and stuffed, stewed, in a pie and with a variety of tasty sauces. Many restaurants offer a 'fresh fish of the day' – you might see *pixxispad* (swordfish), *acciola* (amberjack), *dentici* (sea bream), *cerna* (grouper), *tunnagg* (tuna), *merluzzo* (red mullet), *dott* (stone bass) and *fanfru* (pilot fish) – plus a Maltese speciality, the *lampuka*, which breeds in the Nile delta and is in season from early September until late November. Also available are calamari, octopus, lobster and prawns.

Traditional Maltese Dishes

Aljotta: boiled fish soup with tomatoes and garlic.
Braġoli: or beef olives; thin slices of beef rolled into an olive shape around a mixture of minced ham and pork, bacon, egg and peas.
Fenek: rabbit, simmered country-style in wine, baked or in a stew.
Ġbejna: local cheese made from sheep's or goat's milk, often with peppercorns.
Minestra: a heavy soup with pasta (usually macaroni) and vegetables.
Pastizzi: puff pastry cakes filled with ricotta cheese.
Ravjul (Ravioli): familiar pasta shapes filled with ricotta cheese rather than meat.
Ross il-Forn: baked rice dish with minced pork and beef, bacon, eggs and ricotta cheese.
Soppa tal-armla (Widow's Soup): filling soup with soft cheese, ricotta cheese, eggs, lettuce, peas, carrots and onions.
Stewed octopus: octopus in a sauce of onions, tomatoes, olives and capers.
Swordfish in caper sauce: fried swordfish with a sauce of capers, tomatoes and onions.
Timpana: a golden brown baked macaroni dish with minced beef and pork, eggs, cheese, chicken liver and bacon.
Torta tal-Lampuka (lampuka pie): *lampuka* is a favourite local fish, here accompanied by onions, tomatoes, spinach, olives and capers in flaky pastry.

and the international Pizza Hut chain is represented. For **burger** fans, McDonald's has recently launched itself into the fray.

That the Maltese have a **sweet tooth** is clear from the huge variety of cream-filled cakes and pastries on sale in kiosks and coffee shops. You cannot fail to notice the sweet aroma of frying *imqaret* (date slices with aniseed) or be surprised by the many varieties of *qubbajt* (nougat) at festa occasions. The sweet specialities at Easter are the almond-flavoured iced biscuits called *figolli*. Fresh fruits available include oranges, figs, plums, peaches, grapes and melons.

Fruit of the Vine

Through the introduction of a greater number of quality wines in recent years, Malta is now taken more seriously by wine drinkers. Wines such as Cabernet Sauvignon, Chardonnay, Merlot, Pinot Bianco, Pinot Grigio and Sauvignon Blanc are now found on the supermarket shelves. With Maltese wines, you get what you pay for; wines at the top of the range are good while those lower down, while drinkable, can take some getting used to. Grapes are usually imported from Sicily and the northern and southern regions of Italy.

More adventurous imbibers might try wine from Gozo – powerful stuff with a high alcoholic content that has been known to induce a couple of hours sleep. Local beers like **Cisk** (lager) and **Hopleaf** (pale ale) are good; so is the bittersweet **Kinnie**, a Maltese soft drink now being exported.

WELCOME BAR
DOMINIC
THE HARBOUR
SOUVENIR SHOP

2
Valletta

Valletta is a city which has impressed many people down the years. Sir Walter Scott called it 'that splendid town quite like a dream', to Lord Byron it was 'a city built by gentlemen for gentlemen', while Benjamin Disraeli found that Malta's capital 'equals in its noble architecture, even if it does not excel, any capital in Europe . . . that fair Valletta, with its streets of palaces, its picturesque forts and magnificent churches'.

Nowadays Valletta casts its spell over more than a million visitors annually. It cloaks the finger-peninsula of **Mount Sceberras** between Malta's two great harbours – **Marsamxett Harbour** on one side and **Grand Harbour** on the other – at the centre of the island's conurbation.

Don't Miss

***** St John's Co-Cathedral:** Valletta's incomparable church of the Knights.
***** Palace of the Grand Masters:** the impressive headquarters of the Knights for more than 200 years.
***** Grand Harbour:** see it from Upper Barracca Gardens.
**** A walk around the ramparts:** a leisurely and informative couple of hours.
**** Lascaris War Rooms:** nerve centre of the Allies' Mediterranean fleet during World War II.

History

Valletta owes its defensive character to the **Great Siege** of 1565. It was after the Turks had been repelled at such enormous cost that Grand Master **Jean Parisot de la Valette** decided the Knights should relocate from Birgu into a new fortified city across Grand Harbour which was eventually to bear his name.

The foundation stone was laid with great ceremony on 28 March 1566 by the Grand Master himself. The humbling of Turkish Islam and strengthening of Christianity in the islands encouraged widespread financial support and Pope Pius IV sent his chief engineer, **Francesco Laparelli**, who had designed such a city before the Great Siege, to supervise the work.

Opposite: *Steep, crowded Valletta, with Grand Harbour at its foot.*

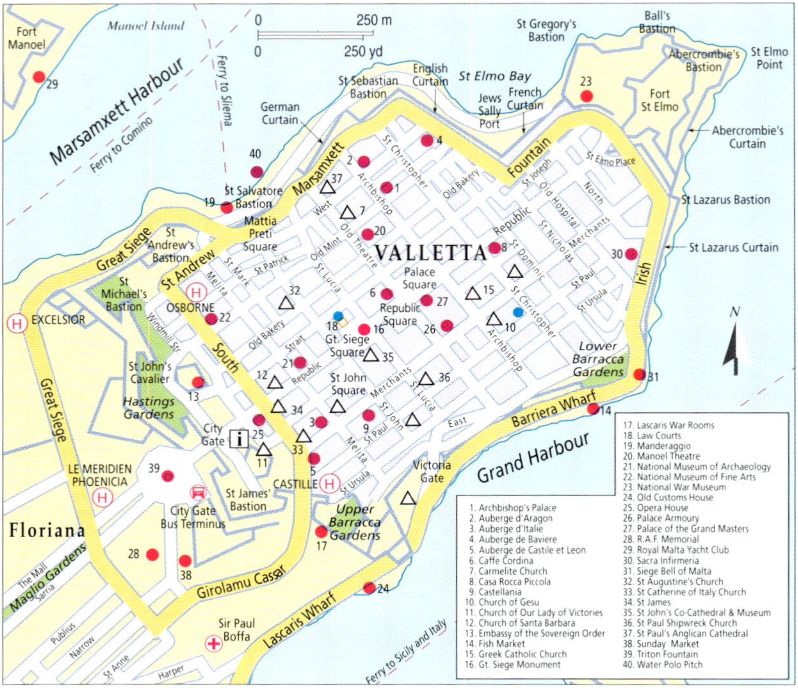

> **SCENIC WALKS**
>
> A walk around the perimeter of Valletta on the road that follows its defensive curtain wall yields views across Marsamxett Harbour and Grand Harbour without parallel. It is a couple of hours well spent and there are open-air bars for refreshment on the way. The trip can also be done by traditional horse-drawn *karrozzin* – the views are just as good and you may be treated to an informative commentary.

A massive work force of Maltese, Sicilians and foreign slave labour was assembled to build the enormous bastions. On the landward side of the peninsula, a ditch hewn from the rock 1km (⅔ mile) long and 18m (60ft) deep added further protection. Within five years the new capital of Malta was born.

Sadly, La Valette never saw completion of his ideal. He died aged 74 in 1568 and building of the city continued under Italian Grand Master **Pietro del Monte**. When engineer Laparelli returned to the Vatican in 1570, the project was overseen by his Maltese assistant **Gerolamo Cassar**, later to design the fabulous Palace of the Grand Masters, the Co-Cathedral and the Knights' auberges. It was in early 1571 that Del Monte decided to move the Knights' headquarters from Birgu to Valletta.

Europe's First New Town

The original ambitious plan for Valletta called for the upper part of barren Mount Sceberras to be flattened and the sloping sides further steepened. But time was critical, money was running short and another Turkish attack was feared. The work never took place, which accounts for the smooth, polished streets of stone steps still found in steeper parts of the city.

Only 1km (⅔ mile) long and 600m wide, Valletta became Europe's first 'new town', designed from the drawing board on a grid pattern. Eight streets run dead straight for most of the peninsula's length, crossed by narrow, stepped side streets which fall away sharply at right-angles towards the two harbours.

The city's clean architectural lines were achieved by strict planning regulations. Houses were of similar design, with no gap between them and with statues at each corner. Incorporated into the plans was space for the Knights' auberges, the Palace of the Grand Masters, the hospital and church of the Order. Despite the severe bombing it suffered in World War II, Valletta today remains both an architectural and cultural delight – a place to be revisited often. Few visitors come to Malta without spending some hours in and around the capital, if only to jostle with the locals and tourists at the Sunday morning market beneath the towering bastions.

Nearby, next to City Gate, is the bus terminus packed with its noisy yellow buses (many of Malta's buses range from old to positively ancient) which connect every town and village with the capital. By day there is a frantic bustle of workers, shoppers and strollers; by night Valletta is left to slumber in relatively uninterrupted peace.

In a city best explored on foot, every street holds fascination. Museums, palaces and churches vie for attention with squares and gardens; and at every turn there is a glimpse of harbour between the yellowing façades.

The Founder of Valletta

The man who gave his name to Valletta, **Jean Parisot de la Valette**, was Grand Master of the Order of St John of Jerusalem from 1557 until his death in 1568. He was a man of immense courage, dedicated to furthering Christendom and destroying the Turks – an objective achieved with the triumph in the Great Siege of 1565. At La Valette's insistence, the Knights remained in Malta thereafter and built the fortified city that was to remain their home until 1798.

Left: *Old yellow buses link Valletta with every town and village.*

Above: *Neptune Court, larger of the two inner courtyards in the Palace of the Grand Masters.*

The Sights of Valletta

Palace of the Grand Masters ★★★

The most highly prized of Malta's palaces is now the seat of the President and Parliament of the Republic of Malta. Every building of the Knights' era was constructed on a grand scale – and the Grand Masters' Palace exceptionally so. However, its impressive, if unadorned, exterior yields no clues to the artistic treasures within.

The inspiration behind the palace was Malta's supreme architect of the 16th century, Gerolamo Cassar. He shouldered responsibility for the building's design and construction in 1571, once the Knights had decided to transfer their headquarters from Birgu across to the newly completed fortified city of Grand Master La Valette.

The palace had started life two years earlier as a house built for Eustachio del Monte, nephew of Italian Grand Master Pietro del Monte. Impressed by the building's focal position on one of the highest points of Mount Sceberras, Del Monte purchased it for the Knights and commissioned Cassar to turn it into a palace.

It was modified by successive Grand Masters until the Order left Malta in 1798. From 1814 it became the British Governor's official residence; since the mid-1970s its mighty walls have contained the office of the President.

The palace encloses two greenery-adorned courtyards. Leave Palace Square through the left-hand archway into the tranquillity of **Neptune Court**, with its bronze statue of Neptune, said to have been rescued from a fish quay in the 17th century. The smaller **Prince Alfred Court** contains a fascinating four-faced clock of 1745 with Moorish figures that strike the quarter-hour.

George Cross Island

A stone panel set in the wall of the Grand Master's Palace on Republic Street commemorates the award of the George Cross to the Maltese people during World War II's darkest days. The citation of King George VI, dated 15 April 1942, read: 'To honour her brave people I award the George Cross to the Island Fortress of Malta to bear witness to a heroism and devotion that will long be famous in history'. The George Cross is now displayed in the National War Museum at Fort St Elmo.

Inside, beside the **marble staircase**, a panel reminds today's visitors of all 28 Grand Masters. Up the stairs are listed Britain's representatives in Malta from 1800 until independence in 1964.

The **Tapestry Room**, formerly the Council Chamber of the Knights, is a magnificent spectacle, with its superb timbered ceiling and set of exquisitely preserved Gobelin tapestries, a gift of Grand Master Ramon Perellos in 1710, which depict mostly imaginary scenes of India, Africa, the Caribbean and South America.

Equally impressive is the Hall of St Michael and St George, also known as the **Throne Room**. Here, too, admire the fine ceiling and the series of Great Siege frescoes painted by Matteo Perez d'Aleccio (1547–1628), believed to have been a pupil of Michelangelo. The decorated gallery opposite the throne is said to have been brought by the Knights when they fled Rhodes.

In the **Hall of the Ambassadors**, in which the Grand Master met envoys, a frieze recalls the Knights' pre-Malta history in the eastern Mediterranean. Canvasses of British royalty add a rather more recent aspect to the **State Dining Room**.

ARCHITECT SUPREME

Gerolamo Cassar (1520–86) was Malta's master architect of the 16th century. As assistant to the Pope's engineer Francesco Laparelli, he helped to plan and build Valletta; when Laparelli returned to Italy in 1570, Cassar took charge. His many fine achievements include St John's Co-Cathedral, the Grand Masters' Palace, the auberges of the Knights, Our Lady of Victories Church and the original Carmelite Church in the capital. He also designed Verdala Palace.

The Armoury **

One of the world's most significant and impressive permanent exhibitions of pre-18th century weaponry and armour is found in two halls within the palace precincts. The most recent weapons are North European air guns from 1800.

The collection of armour includes an Italian-made half-suit believed to have belonged to Grand Master La Valette, the Italian gold-inlaid suit of French Grand Master Alof de Wignacourt which dates from 1615 and a suit said to have been worn by Grand Master Martino Garzes. A group of armour-clad model Knights stands on parade among the display of guns, swords, rapiers, daggers, pikes, lances and other weapons.

Below: *Knights on parade in the Armoury. The fine collection of weaponry and armour numbers some 6000 pieces.*

POSTAL HISTORY

Maltese stamps make an interesting collection – for their portrayal of the country's recent history if not for high monetary values. The first stamps were issued in 1860 and an early halfpenny yellow in pristine condition can fetch Lm 500 today. Various sets overprinted 'Self Government' recall periods when Malta handled its own affairs; up to six commemorative sets are now issued each year. The head of Britain's Queen Elizabeth II disappeared from Malta's stamps with the granting of independence in 1964.

The Auberges ***

An *auberge* was the main base of a *langue*, or nationality, of the Knights. Originally there were eight of them in the city, but now just five of the Knights' headquarters survive. The auberges, mostly designed by Gerolamo Cassar between 1571 and 1590, vary enormously, from the magnificent Castile to the single-storey simplicity of the Auberge d'Aragon.

The **Auberge de Castile et Leon** (the ex-British army headquarters which now houses the Prime Minister's office and is referred to as simply Castile) is one of Malta's finest edifices. It commands the way into the upper city, its Baroque green-shuttered façade dominating Castile Place at the head of the main arteries Merchants Street and St Paul Street.

This was the palace of the Spanish and Portuguese Knights, built originally in Renaissance style by Cassar in 1574 but restyled in 1744 by Maltese architect Domenico Cachia under Grand Master Manuel Pinto de Fonseca. Pinto's bust, with carved banners, arms and Grand Master's crest, is prominent above the cannon-flanked steps at the entrance.

Below: *The Auberge de Castile et Leon houses the Prime Minister's office. The statue is of Maltese writer Manuel Dimech (1860–1921).*

A hundred paces down Merchants Street is Cassar's **Auberge d'Italie**, headquarters of the Italian Knights and until recently Valletta's main post office. Built in 1574, it was enlarged in 1683 for Grand Master Gregorio Carafa, whose bust appears above the door, and at one time housed the Law Courts.

Nearby on Republic Street, the Cassar-inspired **Auberge de Provence**, built in 1575, now houses the National Museum of Archaeology (*see* p. 43). With its façade of Doric and Ionic columns, it was the mansion of France's Provence langue and under British rule was home to the Union Club, focal point of Maltese society. Two other French auberges, the **Auberge de France** and **Auberge d'Auvergne**, were victims of bombing in World War II ; the **Auberge d'Allemagne** gave way to St Paul's Anglican Cathedral in 1839.

The final two existing auberges are both near the Anglican Cathedral. The **Auberge d'Aragon**, a simple single-storey building designed by Cassar on Independence Square, is the oldest auberge, dating from 1571. It now houses the Ministry for Economic Services. The **Auberge de Bavière**, in the former Palace of Bali Carner (1696), looks straight out to sea and housed the Anglo-Bavarian langue throughout its existence from 1784–98.

Above: *The splendid Auberge d'Italie, headquarters of the Knights.*

Buildings of the Knights ***

The Knights' legacy to Malta includes many other outstanding buildings, chief among them the **Sacra Infirmeria**, or Holy Infirmary. The mighty hospital, high above Grand Harbour, was founded in 1574, soon after the Knights' relocation from Birgu, and was remarkably well equipped throughout the Knights' stay.

With the French occupation of Malta in 1800, the Sacra Infirmeria was looted of the silver plate that financed patient care and became a military hospital, a role it continued to play under the British until 1920. Casualties from the Gallipoli landings were brought here in 1915. Medical history was made in 1887 with the discovery of the brucellosis bacteria by David Bruce.

Four direct hits by World War II bombs reduced parts of the infirmary to rubble. Restoration work shelved through lack of funds in 1960 resumed in 1974 and the building reopened as the prestigious **Mediterranean Conference Centre** in 1979. The main Republic Hall and adjacent rooms were rebuilt in 1987 after a fire caused by a laser beam igniting the main stage curtain.

KNIGHTS' HOSPITAL

The Great Ward of the **Sacra Infirmeria**, 155m (170yd) long and 10.5m (34ft) wide, was the world's longest hospital ward. It held 563 beds and could take 914 in times of emergency. Unusually for the time, each patient had a bed to himself with a woollen mattress. Meals for Knights and civilian patients were served on silver plate by the Knights themselves – even the Grand Master fulfilled his obligation to the Order by taking a turn of meal duty.

Shopping Spree

Most Maltese shops are small, family-run businesses which have changed little over the decades. Maltese shoppers head for **Republic Street** in Valletta or for Sliema, while Valletta's **Sunday morning market** below St James Bastion is one of Malta's top tourist attractions – and popular with the locals, too. Pick your way around stalls selling books, music tapes, clothes, household items – you name it and it's there. Along the edge of the market are many stalls with bric-a-brac and second-hand goods.

Cultural gatherings have taken place in the **Manoel Theatre** for far longer – since 1731, when Grand Master Manoel de Vilhena ordered that it be built 'for the honest recreation of the people', with funding from his own pocket. The little box theatre, in Old Theatre Street, is one of Europe's oldest and after years of neglect and misuse has now regained its old glory.

In Merchants Street, opposite the Auberge d'Italie, is the 18th-century **Palazzo Parisio**, Napoleon's headquarters from 12–18 June during the French occupation in 1798. It is now the Ministry of Foreign Affairs.

Streets and Squares **

The city's main artery is **Republic Street**, running the length of Valletta from the City Gate entrance to Fort St Elmo at its northern tip and traffic-free for much of its length. Here are the shops and cafés, crammed together in no sort of order, that give Valletta its social buzz.

In the morning, Republic Street throngs with laden shoppers, besuited businessmen and T-shirted tourists. In early afternoon the city sleeps; shops close from 13:00 until 16:00, leaving only the coffee bars to do business. From late afternoon until the shutters come down at 19:00, the strip teems with life, though with less bustle now as this is strolling time for the young Maltese.

Below: *No cars here: a long street of steps in Malta's capital.*

Just inside City Gate is colonnaded **Freedom Square**, unfortunately used as a car park. Beyond it on the right is the bombed-out shell of the **Opera House**; its truncated columns and lower stonework are all that remains of a once fine building.

Follow Republic Street, with its tiny shops and boutiques shoulder to shoulder with the occasional church or ministry building, past the National Archaeological Museum in the Auberge de Provence on your left, to **Great Siege Square**, with the **Great Siege Monument** by Antonio Scibberas (1879–1947), which is situated

opposite the huge bulk of the post-war, columned **Law Courts**. To the right, as you pass Zammit's colourful flower kiosk, **St John Square** sets off the mighty façade of St John's Co-Cathedral.

Republic Street leads on to **Republic Square**, filled with the bright umbrellas of al fresco cafés. It is a popular spot in summer and you will usually wait for a seat; across the street is the ornate **Caffe Cordina**, established in 1837 in the Knights' former treasury, which has a finely painted vaulted ceiling by Giuseppe Cali and unusual central bar.

In the middle of the square, Valenti's marble statue of **Queen Victoria** presides – more often than not with a pigeon perched aloft – over those taking capuccino and cake. At the back, above the arcade, the pleasing façade belongs to the **National Library**, or Bibliotheca. It was completed around 1796, just before the Knights' exit from Malta, and houses a highly valuable collection of books, documents and manuscripts dating back 800 years.

On display in glass-topped cabinets protected by green cloth are many records of the Knights, including the Processi Nobili documents that proved a Knight's nobility. Fortunately they survived Napoleon's order to have them destroyed during the French occupation.

There is a copy of the act by which Malta and Gozo passed from the hands of Charles V to the Knights and a letter of King Henry VIII, sent from Hampton Court on 22 November 1530, in which he congratulates Grand Master Philippe Villiers de l'Isle Adam on the Knights' acquisition of Malta. In another document, Henry VIII styles himself as Supreme Head of the Church of England and Protector of the Order. Also on show are the original plans of 1721 for the Manoel Theatre.

Above: *Queen Victoria reigns in Republic Square.*

What's in a Name?

When Malta became a republic in 1974, it was time to change the names of many streets and squares in Valletta once again. So Kingsway (formerly Strada San Giorgio, Rue Nationale under the French and then Strada Reale) became Republic Street, Queen's Square turned into Republic Square, Kingsgate (formerly Porta Reale) was renamed City Gate, Kingsgate Arcade became Freedom Square and Britannia Street gave way to Melita Street. Much earlier, the British had rechristened Piazza San Giorgio as Palace Square, a name it retains today.

Immediately beyond, Valletta's main thoroughfare opens on to **Palace Square**, the true heart of Valletta, one side of which is occupied by the Palace of the Grand Masters. Much could be made of the area, which is sometimes used for car parking.

One block to your right is **Merchants Street**, with its family-run shops and businesses which have somehow survived down the years. An upstairs indoor food market offers exceptional fruit and vegetables among a variety of wares; one shop sells nothing but eggs. Another of Valletta's streets of note is **Strait Street**, but for a different historical reason. As the notorious 'Gut', it was packed with hostess bars and dance halls and was a favourite watering-hole of the Navy when the British ran Malta.

Above: *A small store in Valletta. Such family businesses are still common.*

Twin-Tower Style

The twin towers of **St John's Co-Cathedral**, a revolutionary architectural style for mid-16th century Malta that probably derived from Spain, set the pattern for church building in the Maltese islands. There are more than 350 churches and chapels throughout the Maltese islands. Many larger churches have a clock on each tower, one a working timepiece and the other painted on – in the firm belief that this would confuse the devil.

St John's Co-Cathedral ***

The façade is plain, even austere; inside it is sumptuous beyond belief. If Malta's treasures were listed, the Co-Cathedral would easily be at the head. As the former Conventual Church of the Knights, it was granted status as the Co-Cathedral, together with Mdina Cathedral, by Pope Pius VII in 1816.

The church is dedicated to John the Baptist, patron saint of the Order, and is regarded as the finest work of Maltese architect Gerolamo Cassar. The Knights' most important building was created between 1573 and 1577, a priority once Valletta's fortifications had been built and the streets laid down.

One of the two towers facing on to St John Square bears a clock with three faces which accurately tell the hour, day of the week and date in the month. Through the entrance below, the cathedral's barrel-vaulted interior and gilded walls create an overwhelming impression. The oil-painted ceiling, the masterpiece of Mattia Preti, depicts 18 episodes in the life of John the Baptist.

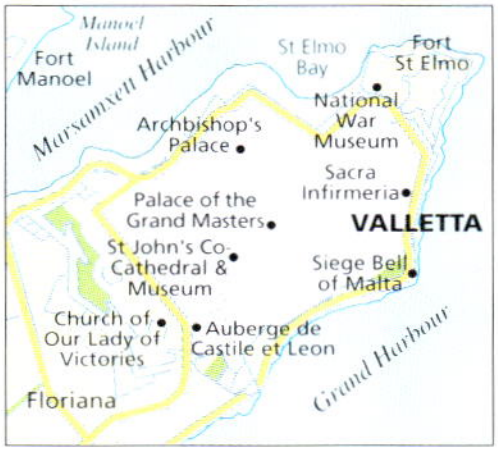

Left: *The plain façade of St John's Co-Cathedral hides a magnificent array of treasures within.*

Almost all of the Grand Masters who served in Malta are buried here. The French Grand Masters L'Isle Adam and La Valette are among 12 entombed in the crypt; others occupy strikingly ornate Baroque tombs in many of the 12 expensively gilded, sculpted and decorated chapels of the Knights' langues on either side of the nave. Others of Maltese nobility lie buried beneath the richly coloured marble slabs that cover the floor.

The silver gates to the last chapel on the right, the Chapel of the Blessed Sacrament, were painted black in 1798 to conceal their real value from the occupying French. The ploy worked and the gates, mistaken for iron, were left while other parts of the church were looted.

The Co-Cathedral's fine Flemish tapestries, based on works by Rubens and Poussin, are kept in the Cathedral Museum and adorn the nave during the Festival of St John in mid-June.

Churches of Valletta ★★★

Valletta's churches are one of the city's outstanding features and some should not be missed out of a tour. **Our Lady of Victories**, Valletta's oldest building (1567), is in Victory Square by the bombed-out Opera House, on the site where Grand Master La Valette laid Valletta's foundation stone. It is attributed to Francesco Laparelli and Gerolamo Cassar and honours the Knights' triumph over the Turks in the Great Siege of 1565. It was given its Baroque appearance in the 17th century.

Malta's Masterpiece

Malta's best-known painting is *The Beheading of John the Baptist*, a masterpiece by the Italian painter **Michelangelo Merisi da Caravaggio** (1573–1610) and his only surviving signed work. It hangs in St John's Co-Cathedral museum; another of his paintings, *St Jerome*, is in the fourth chapel on the left. Both were commissioned by the French Grand Master **Alof de Wignacourt** during Caravaggio's 15-month stay in Malta from July 1607. Received into the Order on 14 July 1608, Caravaggio was imprisoned in Castel Sant' Angelo after a quarrel with a fellow Knight, but escaped by night and fled to neighbouring Sicily.

Above: *St Paul Shipwreck Church recalls the Apostle's arrival in Malta in* AD*60.*

Another of Valletta's first churches, possibly also designed by Cassar, is the **St Paul Shipwreck Church**, commemorating St Paul's arrival in Malta in AD60. The painted and gilded wooden figure of the apostle by prominent Maltese sculptor Melchiore Gafa which stands to the left of the altar is carried through Valletta each year on the saint's feast day, 10 February. The church contains one of St Paul's arm bones and a section of the column on which he was beheaded; it also possesses a prized silver collection.

Also dedicated to St Paul is the neo-Classical **St Paul's Anglican Cathedral**, with its huge, 65m (210ft) spire shaping Valletta's skyline. It was built in 1844 and funded by the Dowager Queen Adelaide, distressed on her visit in 1839 that there was no Anglican church in Valletta. Its site in Independence Square was formerly that of the small Auberge d'Allemagne, built in 1574 and knocked down to make way for the cathedral.

Cassar built most of the Knights' churches in Valletta – such as the original **Carmelite Church**, which was replaced in 1958 after its destruction in World War II by the much larger domed edifice that now rivals the nearby Anglican Cathedral. Others of Cassar's churches were eventually rebuilt and include **St Augustine**, shaped as a Greek cross and modified in Baroque style, and **St Catherine of Italy** (1713), the domed church of the Italian *langue* opposite Our Lady of Victories.

The **Church of Gesu** remains the University of Malta church, although the main body of students was relocated to new premises at Tal Qroqq, above Msida, a quarter of a century ago. It is part of the university building which was formerly the Jesuit College of Studies. In Republic Street near City Gate is the **Church of St Barbara**, where Catholic services are held in English, French and German.

FAITH, HOPE AND CHARITY

These were the names given to the three **Gloster Gladiator biplanes** that alone provided Malta's air cover against the might of the Regia Aeronautica, the Italian air force, at the outbreak of World War II in the Mediterranean in the summer of 1940. The biplanes, which fought alone for three weeks until Hurricanes arrived to replace them, were so effective that one Italian airman estimated the Gladiator fleet at 25 aircraft. Only *Faith* survives, restored and taking pride of place in the National War Museum at St Elmo.

The Capital's Museums

The museums of Malta are fittingly housed in a selection of the country's finest old buildings. As well as viewing the exhibits, visitors can gaze upon 16th-century interiors or, in the case of the National War Museum, enjoy a close look at Fort St Elmo.

Museum Hours

The opening times of the government-run museums vary between winter (1 October–15 June) and summer (16 June–30 September). In winter, opening hours are 08:15–17:00 Monday–Saturday and 08:15–16:15 on Sunday. In summer, museums are open daily (including Sunday) from 07:45–14:00. Admission costs Lm 1; a day ticket costs Lm 1.50, and a weekly ticket (up to 10 visits) costs Lm 4. Gozo's museums open from 08:30–16:30 (until 17:00 in summer) and until 15:00 on Sunday year-round. If in doubt, telephone the government's Museum Department on 230711, 221623 or 239375 for opening times.

National Museum of Archaeology ***

Situated in the Auberge de Provence on Republic Street, the museum contains a priceless collection of artefacts saved from prehistoric temple and tomb sites throughout the Maltese islands. It does a fine presentation job on ancient pottery, sculpted temple stones, figurines, weapons and jewellery – they are particularly interesting if you have visited or intend visiting the temple sites.

Of particular note are the sculpted Copper Age blocks from Tarxien with their spiral motifs – these are the originals; those at the temple site are copies. Watercolours show the temples as they would have appeared and there are detailed models of the prehistoric sites.

National Museum of Fine Arts **

Recognized for its impressive assembly of both Maltese and foreign paintings from the 14th century to the present day, this collection includes work by Mattia Preti, whose Maltese masterpiece was the ceiling of St John's Co-Cathedral, the 18th-century artist Antoine de Favray and 17th-century painter Guido Reni.

The museum is housed in one of Valletta's earliest palaces, dating from 1571 and rebuilt in the 1760s. From 1821 it was the residence of the Royal Navy's commander in chief and known as Admiralty House; among its famous occupants was Lord Mountbatten of Burma, in World War II the commander of the British Mediterranean fleet.

Below: *Malta's Siege Bell commemorates the dead of World War II.*

Siege Bell of Malta

Since May 1992, the 50th anniversary of the George Cross award to the islands, the 8000 British and Maltese who perished in the second Siege of Malta from 1940–43 have been commemorated by the 10-ton bronze Siege Bell which is found beneath its cupola high above Grand Harbour near the Lower Barracca Gardens. The work of English sculptor **Michael Sanders**, it was unveiled during a visit by Queen Elizabeth II and is rung on 15 August each year to mark the lifting of the World War II siege by the Santa Maria convoy.

National War Museum ★★★

Appropriately located in Fort St Elmo, the museum rekindles awareness of the battle for Malta in World War II. Exhibits include the restored Gloster Gladiator biplane *Faith*, General Eisenhower's jeep *Husky*, sections of wrecked aircraft, torpedoes and anti-tank guns. Pictures indicate the extent of Malta's wartime suffering.

The Fortifications ★★

Arriving in Malta by sea, the first landmark you pass entering Grand Harbour is star-shaped **Fort St Elmo** on the exposed tip of the Valletta peninsula. Under massive bombardment, it defied the Turks for 31 days in the Great Siege of 1565. The fort was rebuilt in 1567 and has since been strengthened and enlarged by the Knights and the British; it now houses the National War Museum.

Leading out to Fort St Elmo on both sides of the tiny peninsula are the mighty **curtain walls** behind which Valletta took shape. On the landward side, now separating Valletta from its suburb of Floriana, the defences are strengthened by four mighty **bastions** and are further protected by a wide moat 18m (60ft) deep.

The City Gate entrance cuts through the curtain wall between **St John's Cavalier** and **St James Cavalier**; in all, 11 bastions ring the city. Sections of wall are still known by the langues which protected them – French, English and German Curtain. All around the peninsula there are stunning views out to sea or across the two great harbours; below **St Salvatore Bastion** on the Marsamxett side is the **Manderaggio**, a sheltered inlet used by the Knights.

Below: *St Barbara Bastion and Barriera Wharf, part of the imposing fortifications along Valletta's Grand Harbour shore.*

The Barracca Gardens ★★

Two minutes walk from the Auberge de Castile et Leon are the arcaded **Upper Barracca Gardens**,

a 17th-century parade ground of the Italian Knights with spectacular cross-harbour views. Among the trees and shrubs are a charming sculpture of three children, titled *Les Gavroches*, by Antonio Sciortino, a bronze bust of British prime minister Sir Winston Churchill and a monument to Lord Strickland, an early Maltese prime minister. There is also the tomb of Sir Thomas Maitland, British Governor from 1813–24.

The **Lower Barracca Gardens**, at the bottom end of St Christopher Street, enclose a small Grecian temple monument with a statue of Sir Alexander Ball, civil commissioner when the British took over the islands in 1800. To the left when you enter Valletta through City Gate is **Hastings Garden**, named after the Marquis of Hastings, Governor of Malta from 1824–26.

Above: *The Upper Barracca Gardens, with Valletta's fortifications rising above.*

Casa Rocca Piccola **

This nobleman's house, a short way past the Palace of the Grand Masters at 74 Republic Street, provides an excellent insight into domestic life in the upper echelons of Maltese society from the late 17th century. It was one of Valletta's early buildings, erected for the Knights' Italian langue around 1580, and over the years became home to many top-ranking Knights and a bishop before being sold into Maltese nobility in 1784. It survived the war undamaged.

Today, Casa Rocca Piccola is the Valletta home of the De Piro family; the parents of Nicholas, present Marquis de Piro and Baroncino of Budaq, have an apartment there. It is the only historic Valletta house open to the public and a guided tour takes in the tiny upstairs chapel, bedroom, drawing room, library, sitting room and dining room, all exquisitely furnished.

The Opera House

The bomb-devastated remains of Valletta's Opera House remain a legacy of World War II. The building, designed by **Edward Barry** of Covent Garden fame, was completed in 1866 and immediately took over from the small Manoel Theatre as the capital's leading place of entertainment. Since its destruction in 1942, redevelopment of the site, now used as a car park, has been much discussed – whether to rebuild in the original style or start afresh. Climb the steps off Republic Street to gain an impression of its former grandeur.

Floating Taxis

The traditional way to cross Grand Harbour is by *dgħajsa* (pronounced 'dicer') – Malta's answer to the gondola – the high-prowed, brightly painted water taxi that once ferried Royal Navy sailors back to their ships. Traditionally propelled by a standing oarsman, they now have outboard motors. Many boats are based along Senglea's waterfront, so it may be easier to start a round-trip on the Three Cities side. Annual *dgħajsa* races are held in Grand Harbour on 8 September.

Lascaris War Rooms **

Deep inside Lascaris Bastion, the Malta Command Centre – better known as the Lascaris War Rooms and nerve centre of Allied operations in the Mediterranean during World War II – is an ever-present reminder of Malta's vital role in the defeat of the Axis forces. Within the network of rooms, the war effort was directed by such eminent wartime leaders as Generals **Montgomery**, **Alexander** and **Eisenhower**, Admiral **Cunningham** and Air Marshall **Tedder**.

Here the critical decisions were taken which saved Malta from Axis clutches and set up the Allies' Alamein success. It is presented as a live museum, with 60 or so life-size figures at work in the wireless rooms, cipher room, guns operation room, RAF room and other chambers; each scene is frozen from a particular phase of the war. A personal headphone guide is available and most of the displays are accessible to disabled visitors.

The Wartime Experience **

Malta's wartime history is also recounted in a 45-minute sound and light show in the Civil Service Sports Club on Palace Square in Valletta. Original film footage and still material are used in a vivid presentation of the war effort. There are shows on weekdays (11:00, 13:00 and 15:00) and Saturday mornings (11:00).

Below: *Grand Harbour is a port of call on a growing number of Mediterranean cruising programmes.*

Grand Harbour ***

Arguably the world's greatest natural deep-water harbour, Grand Harbour penetrates inland for nearly 3.5km (2¼ miles) from **St Elmo Point** and **Ricasoli Point** at its entrance to the dockyards of **Marsa Creek**. Focal point of Malta's two great sieges, when it sheltered vast naval fleets, Grand Harbour today sees only limited commercial activity and cruise ships. The cruise traffic is steadily being developed following the building of the cruise terminal below Lascaris Bastion.

From Valletta you can identify (from the left) **Kalkara Creek**, **Dockyard Creek** and **French Creek** below the Three Cities promontories of Vittoriosa and Senglea (*see* p. 59). The **Dockyard**, which employed more than 13,000 men – 15% of Malta's workforce – before Britain's naval withdrawal, now provides work for fewer than 5000, mostly in the ship repair yards.

Grand Harbour is best explored on the 75-minute **Harbour Cruise** that departs several times daily from the Strand at Sliema and also takes in **Marsamxett Harbour** and the creeks of the Three Cities.

Old Customs House *

On Lascaris Wharf, near the remains of a lift that once descended from Upper Barracca Gardens, is the elegant Venetian-styled Customs House of Giuseppe Bonici, dating from 1774. The building is not open to the public.

Floriana

Floriana, a Valletta suburb of ministries, gardens and open spaces inside its own commanding fortifications, has its origins in the 1630s, when it was decided to strengthen Valletta's landward defences against further Turkish attacks. It takes its name from Paolo Floriani, an Italian military engineer dispatched by Pope Urban VIII.

Beyond the land-side curtain wall, with its deep defensive ditch, a second bastioned fortification rises from Pieta Creek and crosses the peninsula to Grand Harbour. The high wall extends along both coasts and is spectacularly floodlit at night. Impressive as the fortifications are, however, they were never

The Granaries

The flat, circular stone slabs dotted about **St Publius Square** in front of Floriana's parish church cover the granaries, vast subterranean pits that served as the grain stores of the Knights. There are similar granaries near the main entrance to **Fort St Elmo**. Grain had to be imported from the Knights' estates in Europe, Sicily and Tunisia to offset deficiencies in the local crop.

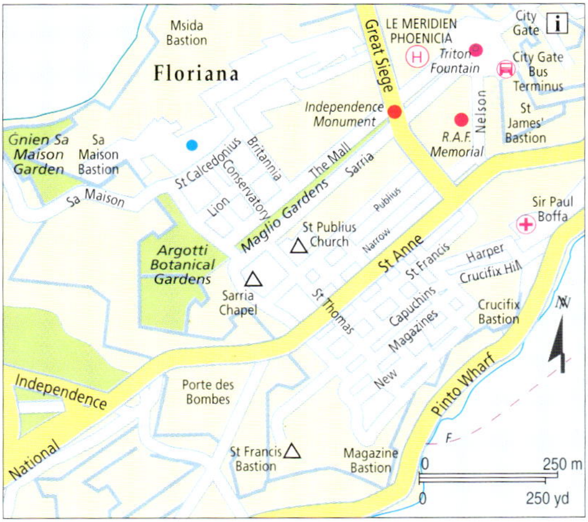

Porte des Bombes

The way into and out of Floriana is through, or around, the imposing Porte des Bombes, a ceremonial twin-arched gateway at the limit of the fortifications now isolated from the curtain wall by carriageways of the main access road. The first of the two archways was built under Grand Master **Ramon Perellos** in the early 1700s to celebrate military success against the Turks; the second archway was added in the same style in 1868.

tested by armed attack. Work began on the streets and buildings of Floriana nearly a century later, in 1722.

Prominent in The Mall, by the Valletta bus terminus from which routes radiate out to every town and village in the island, is the five-star **Le Meridien Phoenicia**, the grand old lady of Malta's hotels.

Churches and Gardens **

Beyond the Phoenicia Hotel and the Independence monument of 1964 are the tree-lined **Maglio Gardens**, once an exercise ground of the Knights, with statues of Maltese worthies. Further on are the **Argotti Botanical Gardens**, created in 1774 and packed with unusual specimens of trees, plants and cactuses from all over the world. Below the Argotti Gardens are the Philip Neri Gardens and a plant nursery. The wide open space alongside the Maglio Gardens is **Independence Arena**, once a military parade area and now a sports ground.

The gardens lead past **St Publius Church**, built between 1733 and 1768 and named after the Roman governor whom St Paul converted to Christianity in AD60. The church, which faces Valletta, was the last parish church built by the Knights. The work of Giuseppe Bonici, it was twice partly rebuilt; further reconstruction took place after World War II. Nearby on a street corner is the round **Sarria Chapel**, built in 1678 to designs by Lorenzo Gafa and containing seven paintings by Mattia Preti.

So close to Valletta, Floriana has had no need to develop as a shopping centre. Small bars and grocery stores serve the town houses either side of arcaded St Anne Street, the main route in from the rest of the island. Among the web of tightly knit streets are the Malta police headquarters and a number of government buildings, among them the Treasury and Ministries of Education and Culture.

Below: *The Porte des Bombes gateway into Floriana. Along with many of the suburb's fortifications, it is attractively floodlit at night.*

Valletta at a Glance

Best Times to Visit

Valletta is best explored out of the peak holiday months of July and August, when there are fewer tourists in town and it is not quite so hot. Malta's capital is busy all year and especially on the feast day of St Paul, 10 February.

Getting There

Buses operate at frequent intervals from all parts of the island to the Valletta terminus at City Gate. Buses operate half-hourly from the airport to Valletta. Those arriving by **car** should use the multi-storey car park outside City Gate, as Valletta's streets are narrow and parking is extremely limited. In summer, a half-hourly passenger-only **ferry** service operates from Sliema – the five-minute cross-harbour journey is far quicker than by road.

Getting Around

Everyone **walks** as driving is virtually impossible around Valletta – most streets are narrow and some, like the main shopping strip of Republic Street, are for pedestrians only. If you insist on having a set of wheels, take a horse-drawn *karrozzin* ride around the city.

Where to Stay

Maltese hotels are graded from five stars downwards; the grading reflects both facilities and price.

Le Meridien Phoenicia, The Mall, Floriana, tel: 225241, fax: 224296. Grand old lady of Malta's hotels, built in 1947. Real five-star sophistication by City Gate.

Osborne, 50 South Street, tel: 243656/7, fax: 247293. Classy three-star in a quiet area of Valletta.

Castille, Castille Square, tel: 243677, fax: 243679. Central position near Upper Barracca Gardens for this modest three-star with its own wine bar.

British, 267 St Ursula Street, tel: 224730, fax: 239711. Run by the same family since 1932, it belies its two-star rating.

Where to Eat

Malata, Palace Square, tel: 233967. Unusual speciality dishes changed daily, plus pasta. Good blackboard menu.

The Carriage, South Street, tel: 247828. Good value; menu of the week is a highlight.

Bologna, Republic Street, tel: 246149. Popular, good-value lunchtime venue with wide Italian menu.

Giannini, Windmill Street, tel: 237121, 236575. Daily specialities support more expensive Italian-style menu.

Scalini, South Street, tel: 246221. Medium-priced steak, fish and pasta menu.

Sicilia, St John Street, tel: 240569. Inexpensive, top-quality lunchtime fish and pasta restaurant overlooking Grand Harbour.

Siracusa, Melita Street, tel: 250652. Shoe-box sized eatery that's good for an inexpensive lunch.

British, St Ursula Street, tel: 224730. Moderately-priced Maltese selection, overlooking Grand Harbour.

Caffe Cordina, Republic Street: traditional coffee-house with vaulted, frescoed ceiling.

Tours and Excursions

Many local tour companies offer excursions from the main resort areas to Valletta. A typical tour of the capital takes in the Upper Barracca Gardens, St John's Co-Cathedral, the National War Museum, Lascaris War Rooms and Palace of the Grand Masters. Sunday morning tours visit the market. Times and departure points vary from company to company. Two operators with extensive tour programmes are Josephine's, 80 The Strand, Sliema, tel: 310435; and Nova Travel Services, Bay Square, Buġibba, tel: 575240, 575960.

Useful Contacts

Tourist information, 1 City Gate, Valletta, tel: 237747.

Police, tel: 191 (general enquiries 224992).

St Luke's Hospital, tel: 234101, 241251, 247860.

Airport (flight enquiries), tel: 249600.

Taxi (24-hour service), tel: 345353, 332074, 345454.

3
Sliema and St Julian's

If size alone determined a country's capital, then Sliema would win hands down. This pleasant seaside resort, much changed over the years, is by far Malta's largest town. It is at the centre of a coastal sprawl reaching from **Pieta**, at the foot of Floriana's towering curtain walls, westwards to **St George's Bay** and embracing **Ta' Xbiex**, **Gzira**, **Balluta**, **Spinola** and **Paceville**.

This is the focus of Malta's thriving tourism industry, thickly spread with hotels, restaurants and bars and catering to the needs of a good proportion of Malta's 1.2 million annual visitors. While Valletta remains the history-laden capital, it is Sliema and St Julian's that present the modern face of Malta.

Don't Miss

*** **Harbour cruise from Sliema:** the best excursion of the Maltese islands.
*** **St Julian's:** one of the most picturesque locations on the island.
** **Paceville:** great for restaurants, bars, and all-action nightlife.

Sliema

Sliema's most notable feature is its **seafront**, stretching for 8km (5 miles) from Pieta to St Julian's past the Marsamxett yacht marinas of Msida Creek and Lazzaretto Creek, Tigne headland and the smooth rocky foreshore lining the Mediterranean. However, the one-time elegance of **Tower Road** running towards Balluta Bay has been lost forever through haphazard planning.

High-rise, glass-fronted apartment blocks have replaced all but a handful of the brightly shuttered stone town houses that once lined this stretch, dominated since the 1960s by the Preluna Hotel, a 14-storey intrusion on Sliema's skyline which until recently had the doubtful honour of being Malta's tallest building.

Opposite: *Msida's creek-side parish church of St Joseph all dressed up for the summer festa.*

THE HARBOUR CRUISE

Malta's excursion *par excellence* is the harbour cruise that operates several times daily from the Strand at Sliema. The trip, with commentary, is a history lesson in itself. It lasts around an hour and a quarter and takes in every creek in Grand Harbour and Marsamxett Harbour. Other pleasure boats leave here for a day trip to Comino and an excursion around the Maltese islands; there are summer voyages on board a three-masted schooner.

The early character of Sliema was shaped in the first years of the century, when the town became recognized as the most fashionable part of the country in which to live. Today, the apartments piled high along Tower Road are the most expensive in Malta. Behind the twisting coast road, it is quite easy to become lost in the maze of densely populated back streets of old Sliema. You will eventually land up at the water's edge again – but most probably not where you expected to be.

The resort's traditional centre is still known as the **Ferries**. From here, steamers once crossed the harbour to Valletta; the service was revived a few years ago and in summer a half-hourly service operates between the capital and Sliema. Pleasure cruises also start from here.

Manoel Island *

The dual carriageway that hugs the shoreline sweeps away from Sliema's pavement cafés to pass the narrow bridge leading on to Manoel Island, now a renowned yachting centre and home to the 160-year-old Royal Malta Yacht Club (like the golf club, it has retained its 'royal' identity from colonial times). Successive plans to turn Manoel Island into a fully fledged tourist centre, with five-star hotels and other amenities, have yet to reach fruition.

At the far end of the island, **Fort Manoel**, now in poor condition, was built between 1723 and 1732 for Grand Master Manoel de Vilhena and could accommodate 500 men. The French garrison were held here in 1800 before being sent home.

The Knights built an isolation hospital for infectious diseases in the early 17th century; the elegant, arcaded **Lazaretto of San Rocco** building, which subsequently cared for World War I casualties, still looks out on the old quarantine anchorage.

Below: *The tightly packed buildings, old and new, along Sliema's waterfront.*

Gzira *

On the landward side is residential Gzira, whose rusting sports stadium just off the seafront once staged Malta's international soccer matches. All important games, including the entire Premier Division programme in the national soccer league, are now staged at the modern Ta' Qali stadium in the centre of the island.

Gzira runs into **Ta' Xbiex**, with a flotilla of ocean-going and smaller craft occupying the berths of Ta' Xbiex and Msida marinas; foreign embassies occupy prime seafront positions and bougainvillea-adorned villas are tucked away among tree-lined side roads. At the entrance to Msida Creek, high and dry on the foreshore, is the brigantine **Black Pearl**, which featured in the 1980 film *Popeye* (*see* p. 101) and is now a restaurant.

At the end of the creek, opposite the well-planted gardens bordering Marina Street, is the dominant **St Joseph's**, parish church of **Msida**, built in 1893. However, if the smooth-rock, Mediterranean foreshore has more appeal – the promenade walk from

Malta's Casino

The colonnaded square building standing well aloof from the buzz of Paceville and St George's Bay on Dragonara Point is Malta's casino. It was formerly the elegant 19th-century summer villa of Marquis Scicluna and his noble Maltese family and is reached through a gateway bearing the Latin inscription *Deus nobis haec otia fecit*, translating as 'God made this haven for us'. The gaming hall, with its roulette, black jack and *chemin de fer* tables, was once the Dragonara Palace courtyard. There is a slot-machine section and restaurant within the casino.

Sliema to St Julian's is always a delight, but watch out for speeding rollerbladers – head inland up the hill from the Ferries, shortly to emerge on the seaward coast. You have cut across the neck of the Tigne peninsula, at the end of which, facing Valletta, is **Tigne Fort**, built on Dragutt Point in 1761 by Grand Master Manuel Pinto de Fonseca to provide cross-harbour cover for Fort St Elmo.

St Julian's ★★★

While Sliema fills more holiday brochure pages than any other part of Malta, it is to St Julian's and, to an even greater extent, its neighbour Paceville that Malta's young people flock each Friday and Saturday night. The two areas have a completely different approach to what passes as nightlife; while Sliema has retained something of its sedate past, along the coast there is an unbridled brashness in the disco bars and fast-food outlets that mushroomed in the 1990s.

However, the former fishing village at the head of Spinola Bay clings on to much of its charm. In summer, St Julian's presents a colourful scene. Brightly painted *luzzu* boats bob in the bay and fishing folk still go about their business – the men unravelling and drying their nets; the women selling the day's catch.

Below: *Spinola Bay at St Julian's, a popular spot for restaurants, still exudes a fishing village atmosphere.*

Some of Malta's best restaurants are here, making use of the pair of fine old arched boathouses that once stood like twin sentinels in the grounds of majestic **Spinola Palace**. The palace, built in 1688 by Paolo Rafael Spinola, Grand Prior of Lombardy, is an architectural masterpiece that itself contains a restaurant. A promenade extends the length of the bay towards the prominent Cavalieri Hotel.

Spinola Bay is but a narrow extension of wider St Julian's Bay; across the bay, on Tower Road leading from Sliema, is **St Julian's Tower**, one of several coastal fortifications erected at the time of Grand Master Martin de Redin in the late 1650s. Situated between Sliema and St Julian's is tiny **Balluta Bay**, with its mini-promenade of palm trees and cluster of hotels and bars. Balluta lacks the buzz of St Julian's; its main seafront features are the Church of Our Lady of Mount Carmel and the water polo pools opposite.

Horse-Drawn Cabs

If the promenade walk from Sliema to St Julian's looks too taxing under the powerful sun, hail a *karrozzin*, Malta's traditional horse-drawn carriage, and travel there in style. There are *karrozzini* ranks at Sliema, St Julian's, Valletta and outside the gateway to Mdina.

Paceville **

Beyond St Julian's, narrow St George's Road climbs from the bay towards Paceville – a stretch of road invariably thronged with holiday-makers and heavy with traffic. Away to the right, the unappealing 22-storey tower dominating this stretch of coastline is the business centre of Portomaso, a new development that includes the 220-room Hilton Hotel, luxury apartments and a yacht marina. The modern Hilton has replaced its stylish namesake of the 1960s; on an adjacent site, the grand 300-room Westin Dragonara Resort has taken the place of the former Dragonara Palace, another 1960s hotel, giving the area a distinctly upmarket feel.

Paceville's half-dozen narrow streets are a mix of traditional town houses,

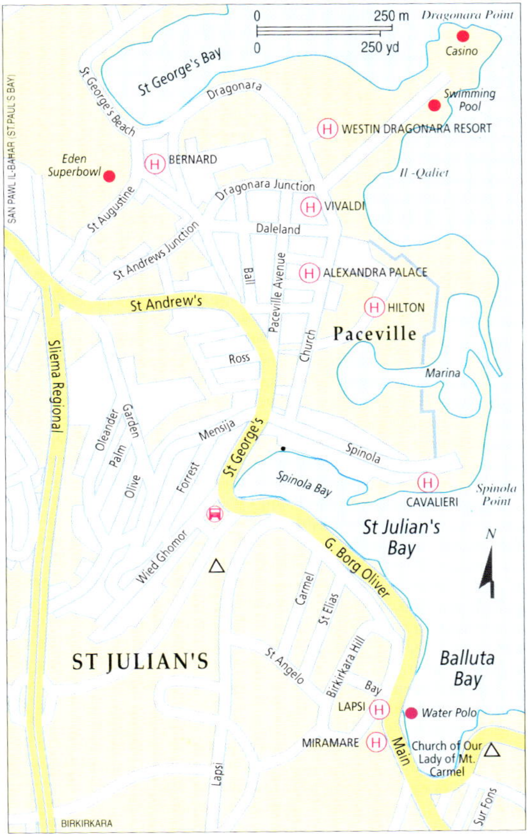

Above: *Water's-edge sunbathing lido and pool of the Fortina Hotel, Sliema.*

hotels, bars and restaurants – fewer of the former and more of the latter as this compact area turns itself over almost entirely to catering for tourists. The range of restaurants is extensive, from Greek to Italian, American to Russian. Out of all proportion to the area is the massive St George's Park apartment complex, Malta's largest with more than 1700 beds catering mostly for British tourists.

St George's Bay **

Development is continuing rapidly past Paceville's neon city and around tiny St George's Bay, which now sports two hotels of the Maltese chain Corinthia Hotels International – the five-star Corinthia San Gorg, built around a coastal defensive tower, and the four-star Corinthia Marina. Around the point is another new five-star hotel, the Radisson SAS Bay Point Resort. The area has another important role to play in Malta's tourism – as the location of the Institute for Tourism Studies.

Both Paceville and St George's Bay were quiet and commercially undeveloped a few years ago. Now they have magnetic appeal for Malta's youth, who arrive in droves for their weekend infusion of disco decibels at a score of neon-lit clubs and bars. Rated among the best discos is Axis. A tenpin bowling centre and 16-screen cinema complex are further attractions.

FESTA COLOUR

Adorning the façade of the parish church with hundreds of coloured lightbulbs is the first stage of every village's elaborate festa preparations. The result is stunning – nowhere more than at **Msida**, where the lights on the parish church of St Joseph reflect vividly in Msida Creek. Then come the decorations – the statues of saints lining every street, the bunting draped from house to house, the flags atop every other building and yet more fairy lights strung between poles. Finally come the car decorations – for the day after the festa, when everyone heads off in convoy for a picnic on the beach.

Sliema and St Julian's at a Glance

Best Times to Visit

The resorts are at their best outside the peak season, as during July and August holiday crowds throng the pavements and finding a restaurant table can be a problem.

Getting There

There is parking for your **car** on the long seafront road or in Sliema's maze of back streets. A half-hourly **ferry** service operates from Valletta in summer. **Buses** operate half-hourly from the airport to Valletta – change at the City Gate terminus for Sliema.

Getting Around

Buses run along the seafront on either side of Sliema; alternatively, pick up a horse-drawn *karrozzin*.

Where to Stay

Sliema

Crowne Plaza, Tigne Street, tel: 343400, 341183, fax: 311292. Attractive five-star hotel in quieter part of Sliema.
Preluna Hotel & Towers, Tower Road, tel: 334001/9, fax: 342292. Four stars; high-rise seafront hotel.
Fortina, Tigne Seafront, tel: 343380, fax: 339388. Malta's first all-inclusive hotel; four stars.
Park, Graham Street, tel: 343780/6, fax: 343770. Four-star near the Preluna.
Grand Hotel Les Lapins, Ta' Xbiex, tel: 342551/8, fax: 343902. Marina-side four-star.
Howard Johnson Diplomat, Tower Road, tel: 345361/6, fax: 345351. Four-star.

St Julian's/Paceville

Westin Dragonara Resort, tel: 381000, fax: 381348. This is an elegant five-star that's a cut above most other top hotels.
Cavalieri, Spinola Road, tel: 336255, fax: 330542. Established water's-edge four-star.

St George's Bay

Corinthia San Gorg, tel: 374114, fax: 374039. One of Malta's newest hotels, offering five-star luxury by the sea.
Radisson SAS Bay Point Resort, tel: 374884. Five-star with great coastal views.

Where to Eat

Sliema

Il-Galeone, Tigne Seafront, tel: 316420, 322695. Good Italian restaurant with range of house specialities.
Mangal, Tigne Seafront, tel: 341046, 343380. Moderately priced menu includes authentic Turkish dishes.
Blondino, Għar il-Lembi Street, tel: 344605. Inexpensive and appetizing seafood.
Pizza Place at Holiday Inn, tel: 343400, 341183. Among the best pizzas in town.

St Julian's

L-Ghonnella, tel: 341027, 315525. Top-quality dining on the terrace of the 17th-century Spinola Palace.
La Dolce Vita, Spinola Bay, tel: 337036, 337806. Lively fish restaurant.
Barracuda, Main Street, tel: 331817, 337370. Higher-priced, quality water's-edge dining in a former summer residence dating from 1793.
San Giuliano, Spinola Bay, tel: 332000. Popular Italian in a former boathouse.
Belfiore, Main Street, tel: 344750. Real Italian with nice views over Spinola Bay.

Paceville

Il Brigante, Ball Street, tel: 311774. Excellent Maltese specialities, children half-price.
Baruffa, Ball Street, tel: 342728, 373840. Higher priced for quality; the display of fresh fish outside is a crowd-puller.
Kolhidas, Dragonara Road, tel: 377456, 336924. Good-value Russian restaurant.

Tours and Excursions

Boat trips operate from the Strand at Sliema, Captain Morgan Cruises, tel: 343373, 331961.
Island Tours are bookable at Josephine's, 80 The Strand, Sliema, tel: 310435.
Dive specialists offering tuition from beginner to advanced level include: Diveshack, tel: 320594; Dive Systems, tel: 319123; Divewise Services, tel: 336441.

Useful Contacts

Tourist information, 1 City Gate, Valletta, tel: 237747.

4
The Three Cities

Look across Grand Harbour from Valletta's ramparts and spread before you is the panorama comprising **Vittoriosa**, **Cospicua** and **Senglea**, known collectively as the Three Cities. Although they are but small towns, they are historically important yet sadly tend to be overlooked by visitors to the Maltese islands.

There are no hotels, restaurants or other tourist amenities in the area, but this lack of late-20th century trappings is offset on the finger-shaped peninsulas of Vittoriosa and Senglea by some fine old buildings that pre-date Gerolamo Cassar's worthy edifices in Valletta. It was around these creeks that the Knights of the Order of St John established their first base on Malta in 1530 following their eviction from Rhodes.

New buildings that went up to accommodate the Knights included auberges for each of the langues and a hospital. New defences afforded some security on the landward side, but Birgu – now Vittoriosa – soon outgrew itself and by the 1560s had overspilled beyond the city walls to create a small suburb. This was called Bormla – now Cospicua (the conspicuous) – linking the other two around Dockyard Creek.

Meanwhile, on the peninsula adjacent to Birgu, the third of the Three Cities was developing as a town in its own right. Senglea, once called L'Isla but renamed after French Grand Master Claude de la Sengle on the completion of Fort St Michael in 1552 was, like its neighbours, destined to play a major role in the Great Siege of 1565.

Don't Miss

*** **Fort St Angelo:** the Three Cities' defensive masterpiece; there are plans to open it to the public.
** **Inquisitor's Palace:** see the courtroom, prison cells and torture chamber.
** **Maritime Museum:** for a fascinating insight into Malta's seafaring past.
** **Views of Grand Harbour:** from Senglea's Gardjola Garden.
** **Cotonera Lines:** dramatic fortification protecting the Three Cities.

Opposite: *Vedette watchtower at Senglea.*

The Knights' Dilemma

Arriving in Malta, the Knights faced two options – to settle inland at **Mdina** or by Grand Harbour in **Birgu**. Neither place met their needs, with Mdina too far inland and Birgu, while better sited, lacking fortifications. The Knights none too enthusiastically chose Birgu, a small town behind **Castello a Mare** (now Fort St Angelo) because it offered shelter for their galleys. It is now called Vittoriosa.

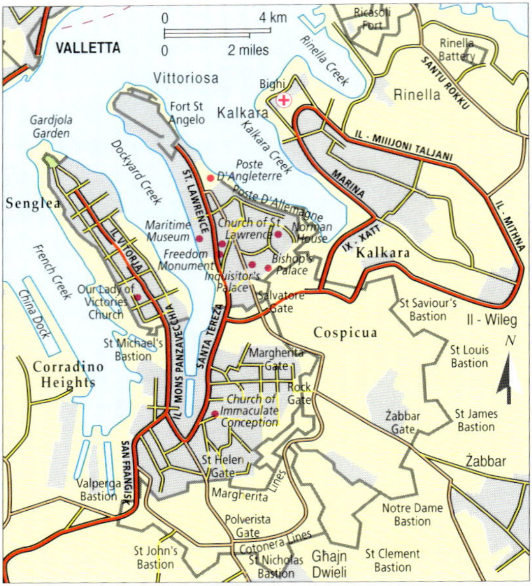

Below: *Mighty Fort St Angelo was the Knights' headquarters in the Great Siege. It commands the entrance to Grand Harbour.*

Birgu was renamed Vittoriosa to commemorate the Great Siege victory (it is still known locally and often signposted as Birgu), but all three cities suffered badly in the mighty conflict with the Turks and when Valletta's foundation stone was laid in 1566, Birgu's days of influence over Maltese affairs were numbered. On 18 March 1571, the Knights crossed Grand Harbour amid great ceremony and moved into their new capital on Mount Sceberras.

With the development of Malta's shipbuilding industry, the Three Cities embraced a new identity as suburbs of Valletta, largely populated by dockyard workers. In World War II, they suffered severe damage from Axis bombers targeting Grand Harbour and the dockyards; Senglea and Cospicua were particularly badly hit.

VITTORIOSA

Fort St Angelo ★★★

This imposing fortress thrusting out into Grand Harbour at the tip of the Vittoriosa peninsula is an architectural masterpiece, and is open for visiting on Saturdays between 10:00 and 14:00. In the mid-1980s it served briefly as a tourist complex; more hours of public access are planned for the long term. The fort was built by Grand Master **L'Isle Adam** soon after the Knights' arrival in 1530 on the site believed to have been occupied by Phoenician and Roman temples. Work involved strengthening an old **Arab** fortification on the site and embracing a mansion of the **De Nava family** and tiny **St Anne's Chapel**, both of which survive.

It became the Knights' headquarters and their command centre during the Great Siege of 1565, when it came under fierce bombardment after the fall of Fort St Elmo across Grand Harbour; its mighty cannon were capable of repelling any seaborne invasion by the Turks. Though restored in the late 17th century, the fort fell into disrepair. Some 350 years after the Knights had made Fort St Angelo their base, it again became a headquarters – this time of the **British Navy**, first as HMS Egmont and from 1933 as HMS St Angelo. In World War II, it suffered some 70 direct hits by bombs.

THE GREAT CHAIN

After Fort St Elmo had capitulated to the Turks during the Great Siege of 1565, the invaders turned their attentions across Grand Harbour to the peninsulas of Birgu (Vittoriosa) and L'Isla (Senglea). But the Knights had in place a defence with a difference – a huge chain, forged in Venice, that was strung across the entrance to Dockyard Creek between Fort St Angelo and Senglea. Evidence of the chain may still be seen below Fort St Angelo.

Inquisitor's Palace ★★

The Office of the Inquisition existed to defend the Catholic faith and counter heresy. As the Pope's agent, the Inquisitor was stylishly housed in a Palace built around 1574. The increasingly ruthless holders of the office were ever unpopular with the Knights and Maltese alike through their abuse of power, yet two eventually became Pope and over twenty more cardinals.

Below: *Carriage of the Inquisitor displayed in the Inquisitor's Palace.*

FREEDOM MONUMENT

On a rocky outcrop before the Church of St Lawrence, the Freedom Monument marks the British naval withdrawal from Malta in 1979. A bugler sounds off as the Maltese flag is raised; the handshake between Maltese worker and British sailor the amicable separation. The ceremony on Vittoriosa's waterfront marked the spot where Nelson's representative General Graham had landed in 1799, initiating 180 years of British military presence.

The palace, built around three courtyards, contains some grand rooms with wooden ceilings. The upper walls of the main hall bear all 62 Inquisitors' coats of arms – though unfilled after 1798, when the Office of the Inquisition was abolished under the French. Visitors can see the graffiti-adorned cells in which prisoners were held awaiting trial and also the execution yard below the courtroom.

Maritime Museum **

Malta's remarkable seafaring heritage long called out for such a museum. The building, the Royal Naval bakery, was designed by naval architect **William Scamp** in 1842 and has a distinctive clock tower styled on one in the British naval yard at Devonport. Vacated by the Navy in 1979, it became a museum in 1992 and includes sections highlighting the Knights, Royal Navy and merchant navy.

The Auberges **

The Knights' auberges in Vittoriosa date from the 1530s, before the Order transferred to Valletta. Seven were built, of which four survive – the **Auberge de France**, **Auberge d'Auvergne et Provence**, **Auberge de Castile et Portugal** in Hilda Tabone Street and the **Auberge d'Angleterre** on adjoining Mistral Street.

The Auberge de France is the oldest and most impressive, built like the others in the style of Rhodes, to where the Knights probably hoped to return. The Auberge d'Angleterre now houses Vittoriosa library. Just off the main square in St Scholastica Street is the Knights' first **hospital**, built upon their arrival from Rhodes in 1530. The stern-fronted building was later used as a nunnery.

Below: *The Maritime Museum with its elegant clock tower by Dockyard Creek. Historic vessels line the quay.*

The 100-Tonne Gun

The mighty Armstrong 100-tonne gun, pointing out to sea above the Mediterranean Film Studios, is the main feature of the newly restored **Fort Rinella**, on the north coast beyond Kalkara. A Changing of the Guard ceremony is re-enacted there from time to time. The entrance to Rinella Battery, less than adequately sign-posted, is midway between the two gateways leading into the film studios.

Left: *The Auberge d'Angleterre, one of four surviving Knights' auberges in Vittoriosa.*

Church of St Lawrence **

This grand building facing across Dockyard Creek to Senglea is a 1691 reconstruction by Maltese architect **Lorenzo Gafa** of the former 16th-century Knights' Conventual Church. In view of its exposed waterfront location, the church was fortunate to lose only its dome to World War II bombing.

The Church of St Lawrence has a rich marbled interior, with well-lit side chapels and paintings of the saint that include Mattia Preti's *Martyrdom* work. There are valuable items shipped by the Knights from Rhodes; in the museum behind the church are Grand Master La Valette's hat and sword from the Great Siege victory celebrations in 1565. The church's large statue of St Lawrence is carried through the streets of the Three Cities on **Saint's Day**, 10 August.

The Gateways *

Birgu's bastions have three imposing gateways constructed in the 1720s. Original road access was by the finely carved **Advanced Gate** and elegant **Couvre Porte**; it now goes through **Provence Gate.**

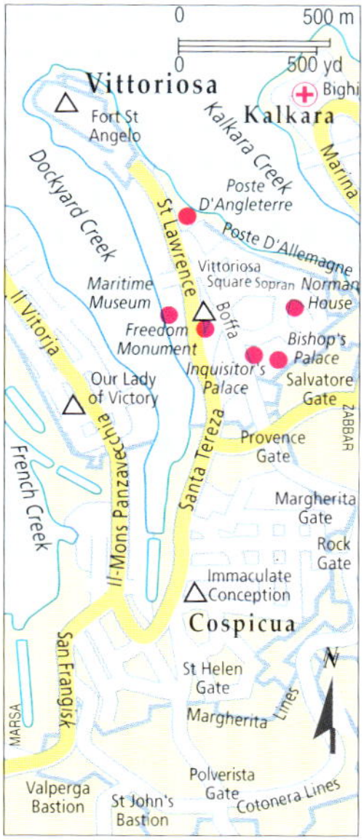

KNOCK KNOCK

The home-proud Maltese take a particular pride in their front doorways, generally the first part of the house to be spruced up each day. Shining brass door knockers can take the form of a hand, a dolphin, an elephant's head, a fish or a Maltese cross; they make excellent souvenirs, as do the locally made porcelain house numbers. Ceramic wall plaques add a religious touch to the front of many homes.

SENGLEA

Senglea straddles the finger peninsula between Dockyard Creek and French Creek, facing Vittoriosa on the seaward side and the Corradino Heights inland. Protected by Fort St Angelo across Dockyard Creek, it developed from the mid-16th century, when French Grand Master **Claude de la Sengle**, who gave his name to the town, dispensed free plots for housing.

On the Vittoriosa side of Senglea, narrow stepped streets fall away to the water's edge; along the other side of the peninsula La Sengle's mighty fortifications extend round its tip into Dockyard Creek and continue inland, forming an impregnable barrier with Vittoriosa's own defences.

Below: *The soaring dome of Our Lady of Victories parish church, Senglea, which has now been restored to its pre-war glory.*
Opposite top: *The fortifications on the peninsula of Senglea by night.*
Opposite below: *An eye for the invader on the vedette watchtower.*

Church of Our Lady of Victories *

Senglea was worst hit of the Three Cities in World War II and the rebuilt town shows little in common with L'Isla, as it was known at the time of the Knights. Among the buildings which suffered direct hits was the 17th-century parish church of Our Lady of Victories in the town's main square. The church was rebuilt by 1957 and interior painting of its dome finally completed in 1995 – a mighty edifice that rubs shoulders with some of Malta's highest-density housing just inside the city's main gate.

Inside are interesting Maltese paintings and a statue of Our Lady of Victories, which is borne through Senglea's streets on 8 September, **Victory Day**, remembering the Knights' Great Siege triumph and the end of World War II hostilities against Malta. The bell tower and dome at the end of Victory Street belong to the **Church of St Philip**, which despite its exposed position somehow escaped the bombing. The work of Maltese architect Carlo Valla, it dates from 1662.

Gardjola Garden **

At Senglea's furthest point, this delightful, newly paved garden on the site of Fort St Michael affords the finest views of Valletta and Grand Harbour. To your right is mighty Fort St Angelo, and beyond the open sea; to your left, the distant derricks of Marsa; directly across the water the cream-coloured bastions that rise to the capital's Upper Barracca Gardens and Castile, flying the flag for the Prime Minister. From here you are in no doubt that Valletta is a fortress city, built to be impregnable. Perched on the tip is the hexagonal **vedette**, a windowed watchtower with carved eye and ear to guard against the enemy.

Cospicua

The town of Cospicua, known as Bormla when it absorbed the overflow populace from the Knights' fortified base of Birgu, today links Senglea and Vittoriosa around the head of Dockyard Creek. The town's clustered streets nestle inside a double ring of bastions built to protect the Three Cities from threatened land attack.

Cotonera Lines **

It was in the mid-16th century that Bormla's growth called for new defences and in 1639 the Margherita Lines began to take shape. Six bastions were planned; three were completed quickly and the others by the 1730s. Work was interrupted when Grand Master **Nicolas Cotoner** pledged to fund an even stronger fortification and between 1670 and 1680 the Cotonera Lines were built, their eight mighty bastions and two demi-bastions strengthening 5km (3 miles) of defences and offering protection for 40,000 people and their animals. Included in the scheme was the construction of Fort Ricasoli.

A Unique Film Set

Close to Grand Harbour, for centuries the hub of Malta's seafaring activity, the modern Mediterranean Film Studios (now called **Rinella Movie Park**) provide movie-makers with a unique sea setting. Two large circular water tanks, cleverly sited to show the sky as a backdrop, have been used in countless films and TV series – *Christopher Columbus* and *Howards Way* are examples. One tank is for surface filming and the other for shooting underwater scenes. The studios are close to Fort Ricasoli.

Fort Ricasoli

Two forts guard the narrow entrance to Grand Harbour – Fort St Elmo at the tip of Valletta and Fort Ricasoli just north of Kalkara on the Three Cities side. Fort Ricasoli was built in 1670 by Italian **Antonio Valperga**, responsible for the Cotonera Lines. Under the Knights, it held a 2000-strong garrison – it is now disappointingly used as an oil storage facility but there are plans to remove the oil tanks. A short distance away is **Fort St Rocco**, one of a number of smaller coastal defences erected by the Knights.

The defences were never tested – with a garrison of 8000 at the time of the French invasion in 1798, the Knights would have been hard-pressed to defend the Lines – and Bormla never grew to fill the enclosed area. Entry into the Three Cities was then, as now, through ornate gateways; impressive still is **Żabbar Gate**, a towering flag-adorned archway on the road from Żabbar bearing a bronze bust of Grand Master Nicolas Cotoner.

Like Senglea, Cospicua was devastatingly bombed in World War II, and much of it was turned to rubble. One building that survived against all the odds was the parish **Church of the Immaculate Conception**, built in 1637 and still standing proud within the close-knit dockyard community.

Below: *Żabbar Gate, the impressive and ornate entrance to the Three Cities.*

Kalkara *

Through Salvatore Gate in the Cotonera Lines and outside the Three Cities, Kalkara hugs the quiet creek of the same name. It was known as English Creek in the Knights' era, when it sheltered galleys of the English langue. More modern than the Three Cities, having been largely rebuilt after World War II, Kalkara is dominated by the mighty façade of **St Joseph's Church**, itself completed in 1956, at the head of the creek.

On the headland of Mount Salvator beyond Kalkara is the one-time **Bighi Palace** of 1832, restored as the administration centre of the Malta Council for Science and Technology. This and the adjacent colonnaded buildings, now housing a school, were developed by the British as the **Bighi Naval Hospital** in the 19th century and remained as such until the British military presence ended in 1979. Beyond the small sandy bay used mainly by locals is **Fort Ricasoli**.

The Three Cities at a Glance

Best Times to Visit

Like the capital Valletta, the Three Cities of Vittoriosa, Senglea and Cospicua are best visited outside the peak holiday months of July and August, when the temperature is more conducive to walking around their narrow streets and enjoying the superb cross-harbour views. Try to be there on **8 September** for the feast day of Our Lady of Victories, when a spectacular regatta in Grand Harbour celebrates the Knights' Great Siege victory and the end of World War II hostilities against Malta.

Getting There

Though the Three Cities are a short *dgħajsa* trip across Grand Harbour from Valletta, most visitors will take the **road** through Marsa, signposted to the Three Cities. Other signs confusingly direct you to Birgu and Bormla, respectively the Knights' names for what are now Vittoriosa and Cospicua. The *dgħajsas* (high-prowed rowing boats more usually motor-driven nowadays) will take you to Senglea and Vittoriosa from Valletta's quayside – negotiate a price with the boatman.

Bus services to the Three Cities include: **1, 2, 6** Valletta–Cospicua–Vittoriosa; **3** Valletta–Fgura–Cospicua–Senglea; **4** Valletta–Cospicua–Vittoriosa–Kalkara.

Getting Around

If you manage to find one, a **dgħajsa** will ferry you across Dockyard Creek between Senglea and Vittoriosa. Once ashore, **walking** is the best way to explore the Three Cities – despite their grand name, they are but small towns easily traversed on foot. There are no taxi stands in the Three Cities.

Where to Stay

There are no hotels, holiday apartments, guesthouses or similar in Vittoriosa, Senglea and Cospicua. Good news is that you are only 20 minutes' drive from Sliema, where there is a wide range of accommodation (*see* p. 57).

Where to Eat

There is very little choice in the environs of the Three Cities. Two **kiosks** with outdoor seating on Senglea's promenade will serve you something-and-chips, but that is the nearest you'll get to *haute cuisine*. The kiosks stay open late, picking up trade after the open-air bingo session ends; they are worth at least a drink, if only for the view across Dockyard Creek to Vittoriosa's floodlit waterfront. There are one or two takeaway **pizzerias**, otherwise small bars frequented by locals might be able to rustle up a sandwich.

For a **restaurant** meal, the best idea is to head west to Sliema or St Julian's, where the choice is extensive. Another option, quicker to reach, is Marsascala, 15 minutes' drive to the east; here also there is a selection of good restaurants.

Tours and Excursions

Half-day **coach tours** from Sliema and Buġibba take in the Three Cities, allowing time to visit the Maritime Museum and Inquisitor's Palace in Vittoriosa, the Cotonera Lines fortifications around Cospicua and Gardjola Garden overlooking Grand Harbour in Senglea. Two main operators with Three Cities tours are Josephine's, 80 The Strand, Sliema, tel: 310435; and Nova Travel Services, Bay Square, Buġibba, tel: 575240, 575960. A two-hour excursion in a 1920s-style **vintage bus** runs twice daily from the Strand at Sliema to the Three Cities, operated by Captain Morgan Cruises, tel: 343373, 331961 or 336981 – an authentic history lesson as the story of the Knights is recounted on board.

Useful Contacts

Tourist information, 1 City Gate, Valletta, tel: 237747.
Police, tel: 191 (general inquiries 224992).
St Luke's Hospital, tel: 234101, 241251, 247860.
Airport (flight inquiries), tel: 249600.
Taxi, tel: 345353, 332074.

F.185

5
The South

This is rural Malta, a patchwork of postage-stamp red-earth fields still tilled by hand and divided by rubble walls; of slow-moving donkey carts and an even slower pace of life. Along its heavily indented coastline are a series of appealing fishing villages, with bays populated by bright red, yellow, blue and green *luzzu* boats. Here too there is the juxtaposition of prehistoric temples and ancient caves beside the modern Freeport container terminal and new electricity generating station, with its obtrusive chimney, which virtually solved Malta's power supply problems overnight when it opened in 1992.

The southern region begins beyond the heavily developed area around Grand Harbour that embraces Marsa and the Three Cities. The small and bustling towns of **Paola** and **Fgura** extend the urbanization towards **Żabbar**; a bypass road sweeps round Żabbar's centre to reach the coast at **Marsascala**.

From Fort St Rocco by Grand Harbour, the rocky shore is deserted save for the tiny settlements of **Xghajra** and **San Pietru**. From Zonqor Point, one bay follows another through **Marsascala** and **St Thomas Bay** to **Marsaxlokk**, Malta's prettiest fishing village.

After **Birżebbuġa** at the far end of Marsaxlokk Bay, high limestone cliffs stretch more or less unbroken for the length of the island, cut only by the narrow, dried-up river valleys leading to **Blue Grotto** and **Għar Lapsi**.

Inland, villages huddle beneath huge churches. The smaller the village, it seems, the larger its church.

Don't Miss

*** **Blue Grotto:** fabulous reflections, but choose a calm day.
*** **Marsaxlokk:** picture-postcard fishing village.
*** **Hypogeum:** unique underground temple complex.
*** **Tarxien temples:** for a peep into the distant past.

Opposite: *Brightly painted* luzzu *fishing boats tied up in Marsaxlokk harbour.*

Above: *An excursion boat enjoys calm weather to explore the Blue Grotto.*

Coastline

Blue Grotto ★★★

Malta's rugged southern coast is pitted with sea caves, of which the Blue Grotto is the most spectacular. The 25-minute boat trip is best enjoyed in the early morning, when shafts of bright sunlight reflecting inside the cave turn the water several shades of vivid blue. Weather permitting, small boats holding up to eight passengers leave the rocky inlet by the fishing hamlet of **Wied-iż-Żurrieq**, with its handful of cafés and souvenir shops at the bottom of a scenic road from Żurrieq village. Though it sounds inviting, the Blue Grotto is in fact too inaccessible for swimming.

By another tiny cove is the small community of **Għar Lapsi**, also at the base of a steep road dropping from the cliff heights. A favourite of the Maltese and largely undiscovered by tourists, it has a no-frills café and good rock scrambles for the kids.

Għar Hasan ★

Hasan's Cave, at the end of a lane above Kalafrana, is entered from a path that affords spectacular views of the blue Mediterranean and has chambers opening on to the cliff face. It is where Hasan is said to have hidden in 1120 after the Saracens' expulsion from Malta. Alternatively, depending on which story you prefer, Hasan was a Turkish pirate who in 1578 took residence in the cave

Luzzu Lore

The *luzzu*, Malta's traditional fishing boat, has a long history – and a colourful one, too. The brightly painted red, blue, yellow and green boats with their high prows are just like the ancient Maltese craft of Phoenician times. The highest luzzu concentration is in **Marsaxlokk**; other luzzu harbours are at **Marsascala** and **St Paul's Bay**. On the bow, the carved eye of Osiris, ancient Egyptian god of the afterlife, supposedly wards off evil spirits at sea.

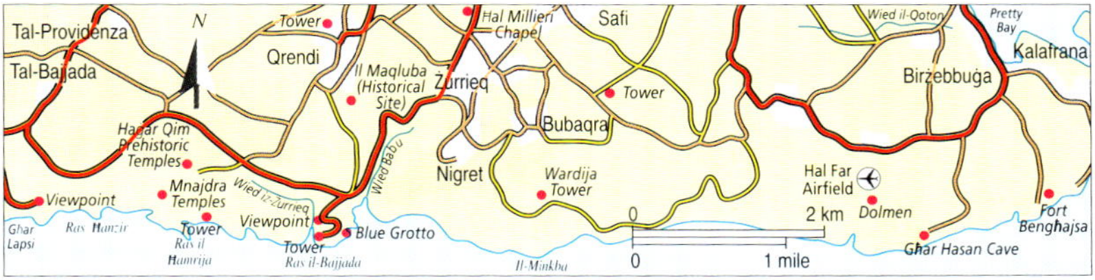

and held Maltese women and girls captive there before they were shipped off to slavery in North Africa. One woman named Mary took the knife to him, thus ending five years of terror, and escaped from the cave – hence the story is there to be told. For a few cents, the lady in the hut by the car park will lend you a torch to see your way into the cave.

All the Sevens...

After Sunday lunch, or in the cool of the evening, village women gather to play *tombla* – open-air bingo. The numbers are called in English rather than Maltese; the cards are well worn, having been used hundreds of times; the counters are usually buttons. The womenfolk perch on ancient benches for their weekly gamble-and-gossip; the stakes are low and so are the prizes.

Għar Dalam ★★

Many of the dwarf elephant and hippopotamus that roamed 130,000 years ago over what is now Malta ended up in this long, tapering cave on the side of a dry river valley above Birżebbuġa. Excavations that started in 1865 have uncovered enough to fill every case in the small museum at the cave's entrance, including elephant molars, deer bones, antlers and hippo teeth. Their discovery fuelled speculation that the Maltese islands were once part of a land bridge between Europe and Africa. Thousands of animals would have perished in the Stone Age cave, with the carcasses of many others washed there by floodwater. Some stumps of stalactites and stalagmites have survived and five distinct geological layers can be identified from the side-lit visitors' walkway running the length of the cave. Recent evidence indicates that the cave was used by Bronze Age man and later by the Phoenicians.

Below: *Exploring the depths of Għar Dalam, the 'cave of darkness'.*

Try Two Wheels

If you are in Malta outside the hottest months, consider hiring a **bike** to do your sightseeing – it's a good way to get off the beaten track on lanes and tracks in the south of the island that are often inaccessible to cars. The all-terrain machines now available are particularly suited to Gozo's more remote parts. Cyclists should equip themselves with a decent map, as signposting is scarce or non-existent away from the towns and villages; distances are never given.

Tarxien Temples and Hypogeum

The three Tarxien temples, believed to date from between 3000 and 1800BC, are among the most important evidence of the ancient cultures that once inhabited Malta. The temple site, now engulfed by urbanization, was discovered by a farmer in 1915.

In the first temple is a replica (the originals are in the National Museum of Archaeology in Valletta) of the base of a giant goddess statue, one of the world's earliest known representations of a deity. The second temple, with three chambers on either side of a central passage, is thought to have been used for the initiation of priests; it includes carvings of a bull and a sow with litter. Stone balls used to roll the massive temple slabs into place can also be seen. Early forms of cremation took place within these walls, evidenced by the darkly discoloured stone.

Ħal Saflieni Hypogeum ★★★

Malta's unique underground temple complex, discovered by chance in 1902 when builders were preparing a housing site in Paola, comprises a labyrinth of corridors and chambers on three levels, cut from the soft limestone between 4000 and 5000 years ago.

Below: *An aerial view of the Mnajdra temple site clearly shows the shape of the three temples.*

The upper level, 6m (20ft) below ground, dates from 3000BC; the other two levels, to a depth of 12m (40ft) at the foot of a modern staircase, were built around 2000BC to resemble surface temples elsewhere and so feature more ornate ceilings, walls and doorways. This was a place of both ancient worship and burial and at its lowest level the complex was found to contain a burial chamber with the remains of 7000 bodies.

The Holy of Holies chamber has strong architectural features and the red colouring of death on its walls – it was probably a shrine for the sacrifice of animals. Another, the oracle chamber, has outstanding acoustics and will reverberate a male – but not female – voice around its walls.

Haġar Qim and Mnajdra ★★

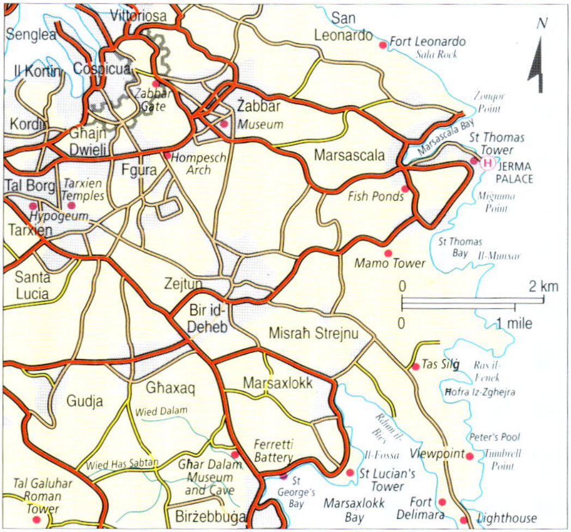

High on the southern clifftop between Għar Lapsi and the Blue Grotto, close to the village of Qrendi, are two more prehistoric temple sites. Haġar Qim, first excavated in 1839, occupies the higher ground; Mnajdra is a short way down the slope. Both face the open sea across to the islet of Filfla, which possibly had a ritualistic role in temple life that would explain the temples' remote location.

Haġar Qim (its simple translation is 'standing stones') used some of the largest slabs found in Maltese temple building, one a massive 7m by 3m (22ft by 10ft). The blocks were transported on the stone balls unearthed in some temples, but archaeologists remain baffled by how the larger ones were placed in their upright position. Haġar Qim's soft globigerina limestone walls have weathered badly, however, and later temple builders used the harder coralline limestone.

Mnajdra's three temples, within their protective coralline limestone wall, are in a better condition than Haġar Qim. The temples, dating from 2500BC, feature good corbelling and decorative work; a square-holed oracle chamber which was used by the priest can be clearly made out.

Marsascala ★★

The development of Marsascala from fishing village into small holiday resort followed the opening of the Jerma Palace Hotel around the headland in 1982. At that time a handful of waterfront bars and a couple of restaurants met the needs of day trippers; since then many more

Isle of Filfla

Filfla, 5km (3 miles) offshore, is Malta's smallest island, measuring just 280m (910ft) by 50m (160ft) across its plateau. Sheer cliffs rising to 60m (195ft) render it inaccessible to all but experienced rock climbers. A small chapel existed on Filfla from the 14th to the 16th centuries; until 1971 the island was used for target practice by British warships and there are still unexploded bombs around its base. Since 1988 Filfla has been a Nature Reserve, with breeding colonies of the storm petrel, herring gull, Cory's shear water and Manx shearwater.

The Seasick Summit

Marsaxlokk Bay hosted one of the most remarkable meetings between heads of state in modern times. Here, aboard a naval ship, the **Bush–Gorbachev** summit between the Soviet and US leaders symbolically ended the Cold War, having been switched from Valletta for security reasons. In rough weather, the meeting dubbed the 'seasick summit' was held in the bay between the Freeport and the power station on 2–3 December 1989. An ugly monument on Birżebbuġa seafront, paint-splattered and already badly weathered, commemorates the historic occasion.

have opened to cater for the rash of holiday apartments spreading towards St Thomas Bay. Now it is a popular night venue for the Maltese, who drive from all parts of the island at weekends to eat, drink and soak up the music. Despite the building work, a wide promenade and recently imposed one-way traffic system, Marsascala clings on tenuously to its village atmosphere – a world apart from Sliema, St Julian's and, further up the coast, St Paul's Bay. The tranquillity, however, may not last much longer.

Next to the distinctive Libyan-owned Corinthia Jerma Palace Hotel – where Libyan leader Colonel Ghadaffi was an early visitor – is **St Thomas Tower**, built in 1614 by Grand Master Alof de Wignacourt after the Turks had landed in Marsascala Bay and sacked Żejtun. The fort, which was never attacked, was abandoned in 1798 when Malta fell to the French and has latterly seen use as a restaurant.

The coast road leads on to **St Thomas Bay**. Though villas and apartments edge the road, the bay with its outdoor café and stone fishermen's huts has remained largely unchanged over the years.

Below: *Fishermen on the quay at Marsaxlokk.*
Opposite: *Pretty Bay.*

Marsaxlokk ★★★

While Marsascala has grown considerably to meet the increasing needs of tourism, only in recent years has Marsaxlokk made any such concessions. Thankfully, there are still no hotels or bland apartment blocks to disfigure Malta's most charming seaside village – just a scattering of fish restaurants and a few seafront bars that cater mainly for the many day trippers in the area.

Marsaxlokk (a corruption of the words for 'harbour' and 'sirocco', the warm winter wind that blows up from the Sahara) overlooks a bay packed in summer with traditional high-prowed *luzzu* fishing boats. Along the quayside, the Sunday morning market, selling everything from locally made lace tablecloths to freshly caught octopus, awakens the neighbours early and throughout the day attracts a succession of coach parties. South of the village, the early 17th-century St Lucien Tower, another Knights' stronghold, is now a marine laboratory.

Birżebbuġa *

A favoured landing place for enemy fleets in centuries past – the Turks before the Great Siege of 1565 and the French to terminate the Knights' rule in 1798 – Birżebbuġa has long been a summer resort for the Maltese. A lack of quality hotels and decent restaurants has isolated this small town from mainstream tourism. Dwarf palm trees fringe **Pretty Bay**, the south's only sandy beach of note, though thanks to the proximity of the Freeport it hardly justifies the name nowadays.

The resort spreads from compact **St George's Bay**, with small boats clustered behind its breakwater, through Pretty Bay to **Kalafrana** at the entrance to the vast **Malta Freeport** container terminal, which now processes some half-million containers annually. Near the most southerly point on the island is the redundant **Ħal Far Airfield**, a legacy of World War II, now used for speed trials by motor enthusiasts.

Coastal Walks

While Malta's rocky foreshore is not ideal for serious hiking, there are good road walks along the coast. One from Valletta will take you past both Floriana and Marsamxett Harbour to Sliema and then St Julian's and St George's Bay. Another, from Marsascala, passes St Thomas Tower and St Thomas Bay before crossing the Delimara peninsula to Marsaxlokk; from here you can walk on to Birżebbuġa.

Southern Villages

Żurrieq, one of Malta's oldest parishes, is on the road to the Blue Grotto. The parish church of St Catherine dates from 1634 and contains fine works by Mattia Preti, who lived in the village in 1675. Several buildings from the Knights'

Above: *Festa time in Żurrieq. Flags and banners adorn the streets by St Catherine's parish church.*

era include the Armeria Palace, a former armoury. The medieval Church of the Annunciation was built on the site of the long-abandoned Ħal Millieri settlement.

Nearby **Qrendi** has three churches – the parish church of Santa Maria by Lorenzo Gafa (1685); St Catherine Tat-Torba, with its unusual façade added to an existing nave (1625); and St Saviour's, built in the style of a chapel. Near the latter is the Knights' late 16th-century Gwarena Tower, Malta's only octagonal defence.

Luqa, the site of Malta International Airport, was almost destroyed in World War II. The rebuilt parish church of St Andrew, originally dating from 1650, contains a Mattia Preti altarpiece. Nearer the new terminal is **Gudja**, birthplace of the architect Gerolamo Cassar, with the isolated **St Mary Ta' Bir Miftuħ**, dating from 1430 and one of the original 10 parish churches of Malta.

The road east from Gudja passes through **Għaxaq** to **Żejtun**, dominated by Lorenzo Gafa's massive parish church of St Catherine, the dome of which can be seen from afar. Much older is the former parish church of St Gregory, built in 1436 and enlarged by the Knights; the remains of more than 80 victims of a Turkish attack were discovered in passages there in the 1960s.

Żabbar, on the site of the camp established by the Turks before the Great Siege of 1565, boasts one of Malta's most unorthodoxly beautiful churches in the Sanctuary of the Virgin of Grace. This is Maltese Baroque at its most ornamental. It was started in 1641 and work continued over the next 100 years or so – hence some lack of harmony in design. On a roundabout on the Fgura side of town is the Hompesch Arch dedicated to the last Grand Master, Ferdinand de Hompesch.

Building Blocks

All over Malta and Gozo, the buildings are of the same material – the pale yellow globigerina limestone quarried mostly to the north of **Qrendi** and **Mqabba**. Demand is high, with building of new homes and hotels going on apace. The sheer sides of the quarries are due to the soft limestone, which hardens with age, being cut rather than blasted. Infilling takes place when a quarry closes so that the countryside does not remain disfigured for longer than is necessary.

The South at a Glance

Best Times to Visit

Malta's southern part is best seen in **late spring**, if only for appreciating the island's greenery and admiring the wild flowers that colour the countryside between the scattered villages. It is amazing how quickly the scorching summer sun turns the landscape several shades of brown.

Getting There

The southern areas of Malta are within easy reach of the Valletta–Sliema conurbation and roughly a half-hour's drive by **car** from the St Paul's Bay resort area. A large number of **bus routes** serve different parts of the area.

Getting Around

A comprehensive **road** network links the towns and villages of Malta's south. Signposting has improved in the last year or two, but should you stray from the main roads, work out which direction you want to go and steer by the sun! A road tunnel beneath Malta International Airport's main runway links the communities north and south of the airport. The only road access to the sea on the southern coast is at Wied-iż-Żurrieq and Għar Lapsi. **Bus services**, mostly linking towns and villages in the area with Valletta, offer good connections around the region.

Where to Stay

Corinthia Jerma Palace, Dawret it-Torri, tel: 633222, fax: 639485. Biggest and best in the south; distinctive four-star situated next to the sea on the edge of Marsascala.
Etvan, Bahhara Street, tel: 633265, fax: 684330. New three-star hotel near the centre of Marsascala.

Where to Eat

Hunters' Tower, Wilga Street, Marsaxlokk, tel: 651356. More expensive seafront restaurant with good fish dishes and an excellent range of starters.
Fisherman's Rest, St Thomas Bay, tel: 632049, 681763. Unpretentious and off the tourist track, it is inexpensive and hard to beat for seafood.
Sottovoce, Marina Prominade, Marsascala, tel: 632669. Good value Mediterranean; menu includes 24 pasta dishes.
Langustini, Triq Id-Dahla, Ta' San Tumas, tel: 687590. Large rooftop signage identifies long-established quality fish restaurant near St Thomas Bay.
Red Lobster, Triq Il-Qaliet, Marsascala, tel: 687322. Fish menu (and lobster, of course).
L'Awwista, Zonqor Road, Marsascala, tel: 632022. Mid-priced fish specialities overlooking the bay.
San Tomaso, St Thomas Bay, tel: 639394. Al fresco dining in summer; excellent lunchtime pasta. A good spot to end your holiday.
Pisces, Xatt is-Sajjieda, Marsaxlokk, tel: 684956. This restaurant is modern in style and has a splendid and inexpensive fish menu.
Is-Sajjied Restaurant, Xatt is-Sajjieda, Marsaxlokk, tel: 682549. Serves a good antipasti selection and also fresh fish, mid-priced.

Tours and Excursions

Half-day and full-day **coach tours** from Sliema and Buġibba take in Malta's south, visiting Wied-iż-Żurrieq for boat trips to the Blue Grotto and the colourful fishing village of Marsaxlokk with its open-air market. The trips usually take in Marsascala and Birżebbuġa and visits the stone quarries near Mqabba. Longer excursions visit the ancient temple sites at Tarxien and the prehistoric Għar Dalam cave. Leading operators with tours to the south are Josephine's, 80 The Strand, Sliema, tel: 310435; and Nova Travel Services, Bay Square, Buġibba, tel: 575240, 575960.

Useful Contacts

Tourist information, 1 City Gate, Valletta, tel: 237747.
Police, tel: 191 (general inquiries 224992).
St Luke's Hospital, tel: 234101, 241251, 247860.
Taxi, tel: 345353, 332074.
Airport (flight inquiries), tel: 249600.

6
Mdina and Rabat

Mdina was established by the Romans on a Bronze Age site as a settlement called **Melita** (meaning 'honey'), which was later fortified and renamed el-Medina ('city') by the Arabs. By the 16th century, after it had seen off Saracen raids, Mdina was the most sought-after place to live on Malta. High on a ridge in the centre of the island, it was easy to defend, while fertile land at its base provided food for those within. At the time of the **Great Siege** in 1565, it was the headquarters of the cavalry and when a force of 200 men rode forth from the city they were thought by the Turks camped at Marsa to be the feared reinforcements from Sicily – an error of judgement that led to the Turks' retreat and eventual downfall.

The Knights' decision to build Valletta as their new capital after the Great Siege diminished Mdina's importance – from being Citta Notabile, or Eminent City, it became Citta Vecchia, the Old City. Much later it became known as the **Silent City**, its narrow streets and alleyways uncluttered by motor cars, which are banned to all but residents.

At only 4ha (10 acres), Mdina is a city to wander in. Nowhere can so much rich history be packed into so small an area – palaces, a cathedral, churches, museums, a convent, small piazzas and houses of the Maltese aristocracy squeezed together inside the sturdy fortified walls and further protected by an enclosing dry moat. From the walls, the panorama across half of Malta to

Don't Miss

***** Mdina's Cathedral:** a masterpiece in Maltese Baroque architecture.
***** A stroll in Mdina:** the best way to see the city – cars are banned anyway.
***** Rabat's Catacombs:** rock-cut burial chambers of the early Christians.
* Tea at the **Fontanella tea garden:** an unrivalled setting.

Opposite: *From flowering fields in the centre of Malta rises the unmistakable shape of the city of Mdina.*

Malta's Aqueduct

The stone arches that appear intermittently along the road from Ħamrun towards Rabat are all that is left of the 17th-century Wignacourt Aqueduct, one of Malta's great engineering feats. The 15km (9½ mile) aqueduct, built to carry water from the Mdina heights to Valletta, was built between 1610 and 1616 and named after Grand Master **Alof de Wignacourt**, who financed the project.

Above: *The ancient walls and spires of Mdina's skyline, dominated by the cathedral.*
Below: *The clock and bell tower on the cathedral.*

Grand Harbour and the Mosta Dome is unsurpassed. The city's own distinctive profile is Malta's crowning point, visible from much of the island.

Expansion beyond the city walls created the present town of **Rabat**; with its catacombs and Roman remains, it is older than Mdina and probably dates back to the Phoenicians. Rabat is the busy commercial hub of central Malta, with shops, bars and restaurants – and a marked contrast to the silent and brooding museum piece that is Mdina.

The Cathedral ★★★

One of Malta's treasures, Mdina's Baroque cathedral is dedicated to St Paul and shares the title of Co-Cathedral with St John's in Valletta. It was erected between 1697 and 1702 after the 1693 earthquake had all but destroyed the 13th-century original.

The distinguished Maltese architect **Lorenzo Gafa**, who strengthened and rebuilt parts of the old cathedral shortly before the earthquake struck, designed the new building that was to prove his masterpiece.

Within the grand and gilded interior, the many-coloured marble floor tablets, which identify the graves of important social and religious figures, are reminiscent of St John's Co-Cathedral. The apse, survivor of the earthquake with its 'Shipwreck of St Paul' mural by **Mattia Preti**, found a place in the new cathedral; also saved from the earthquake were the marble font and oak sacristy door.

High point in every respect is the cathedral's striking dome, a readily recognizable feature of the Mdina skyline, and widely regarded as Gafa's finest work. The inside of the dome was painted by **Mario Caffaro Rore** in 1955.

The cathedral's fine interior decorations include the nave ceiling fresco of 1794 by two Sicilian brothers, **Antonio** and **Vincenzo Manno**, depicting the life of St Paul. Other treasures are the Madonna icon, which some take to be the work of St Luke, in a side chapel; a silver medieval processional cross believed to have been brought by the Knights from Rhodes; and a communion chalice supposedly used by St Paul. The two early-17th century bronze cannon formally guarding the cathedral's entrance were returned to Malta from London at the insistence of the Governor in 1888.

MALTESE CHRISTMAS

The Maltese people make a lot of Christmas, dressing their houses and streets elaborately for the festive season. Nativity scenes adorn many front windows; cress is traditionally planted around the base of a crib containing a porcelain baby Jesus. In the south of the island, illuminated orange folded paper stars are hung in upstairs bay windows, their light glowing against a back curtain. Streets and churches in the towns and villages are hung with coloured lights that include the Maltese 'shooting star' decoration; many parishes have their own crib scene.

Cathedral Museum **

Many artefacts salvaged after the earthquake are on display in the cathedral museum, which is housed in the seminary across Archbishop Square to the right of the cathedral. The building, a departure in style from other buildings of the period, is attributed to both Giovanni Barbara and Andrea Belli and dates from 1733.

In the museum are silver statues, outstanding Dürer engravings, paintings, manuscripts, lace and some 15th-century Sicilian choir panels.

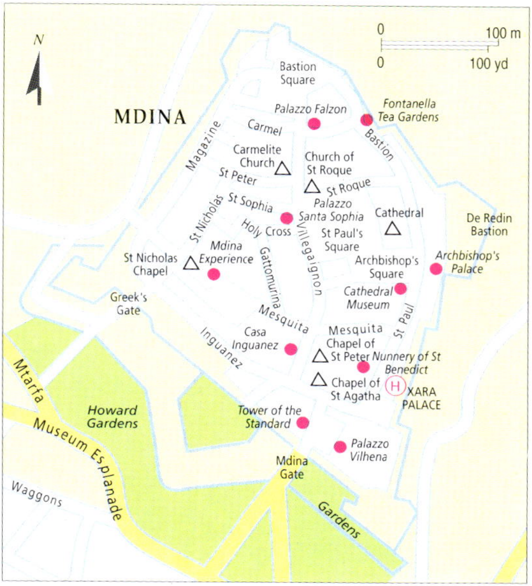

NORMAN HOUSE

On Villegaignon Street, near the Carmelite Church, is the restored **Palazzo Falzon**, with a slit-windowed lower section which dates from the 14th century. Sometimes called the **Norman House**, it is the only private house in Mdina open to the public and functions as a museum with a good display of antiques, paintings and furniture.

Above: *The courtyard of the Palazzo Falzon, a former nobleman's house.*
Below: *The labyrinthine alleyways of Mdina.*
Opposite: *Mdina Gate, the main entrance into the Silent City.*

AROUND MDINA

Streets, Walls and Gates

The walls enclosing Mdina and giving the Silent City its fortress appearance have their origins in Roman, Byzantine, Arab and Norman history, though it was the Knights who gave them their present form. The Arabs cut the ditch, today planted with orange trees, which the Knights widened into a dry moat that effectively isolated the citadel and cut Mdina to a third of its original size.

It was after the Great Siege and the development of Valletta that the Knights turned their attentions to the old capital. There are three ways into the city – through **Mdina Gate**, past the horse-drawn *karrozzini* standing for hire on the Rabat side of the bridge; via **Greeks' Gate** leading from the moat at the far end of Howard Gardens; and through a hole in the wall on the west side. The latter was cut early this century to give Mdina's citizens a short cut to the new railway station below the walls; the railway, alas, no longer exists.

The ornamental Baroque archway of the Mdina Gate took

its present from under Grand Master Manoel de Vilhena in 1724. The original access was at night across the drawbridge. At the same time the Greek's Gate, taking its name from the small Greek community who lived in the area, was similarly enhanced.

Mdina's main thoroughfare, **Villegaignon Street** – named after the French knight Nicolas Durand de Villegaignon (1510–71), who founded Rio de Janeiro – cuts from Mdina Gate to the high ramparts on the north side and is lined by most of the city's finest houses. To left and right as you amble through the quiet city, whose population of fewer than 400 rarely appear to venture outdoors, are narrow streets and gently curving alleyways, so designed to protect the inhabitants from attack and the buildings from the strong summer sun.

The street opens out into **St Paul's Square** before the great cathedral. Here there is a red telephone kiosk and postbox, legacies of British rule which show up brightly against the yellow stonework. Found at the far end of Villegaignon Street, behind the bulwark, is bougainvillea-flanked **Bastion Square**, with superb views across the Maltese landscape to St Paul's Bay, Grand Harbour and, in the middle distance, Mosta Dome and the new National Stadium.

Malta's Railway

Malta enjoyed a brief flirtation with the railway age. The Malta Railway Company was formed in 1880 and on 1 March 1883 it opened a line between Valletta and Mdina. Traffic was poor, however, and the Maltese administration took over the line in 1890. It ran profitably until competition from the Valletta–Birkirkara tramway, which started up in 1905, and buses caused its demise. Planned extensions to Sliema, Mosta and Żebbuġ never materialized and, unable to sustain further losses, the railway closed on 1 April 1931.

A Stroll in the Silent City ***

Entering through **Mdina Gate**, immediately on the right is the **Palazzo Vilhena**. It began life as the Magisterial Palace and was the inspiration of Maltese architect Giovanni Barbara in 1733; in 1909 it became the Connaught Hospital of the British and is now the **Museum of Natural History**.

To the left, the reassuring blue lamp of Mdina police station hangs from the 16th-century **Tower of the Standard**. Its

DARKEST MDINA

- Below the Palazzo Vilhena in a labyrinth of rooms and passages, the **Mdina Dungeons** recreate Malta's less savoury past in a series of tableaux. **Tales of the Silent City**, on Villegaignon Street, is a similar tableau attraction; the **Knights of Malta** likewise in Magazine Street by the city wall.
- In a house on Mesquita Square, the multi-lingual **Mdina Experience** audio-visual show, similar to the Malta Experience at the Mediterranean Conference Centre in Valletta, provides an insight into the Silent City.
- The Palazzo Costanzo of the Knights on Villegaignon Street recreates the life, sounds and smells of 14th- and 15th-century Maltese life in an exhibition that is called **Medieval Times**.

function has always been to protect the populace – originally fires were lit aloft to warn the citizens of an impending invasion. Directly ahead across **St Publius Square** is **St Peter's Monastery**, home of the Benedictine nuns, rebuilt in 1625 but 200 years older. The nuns are of a strict order that decrees they must be buried within the precincts; the only men allowed inside are the doctor, decorator, lawyer and undertaker – and then only with the bishop's permission.

Opposite the nunnery, at No. 3 Villegaignon Street, is imposing **Casa Inguanez**, the home since 1350 of Mdina's oldest family and once the hereditary governors of the city. The oldest house in Mdina – and reputedly in Malta – is **Palazzo Santa Sophia**, found on the left hand side of Villegaignon Street just past the cathedral by Holy Cross Street.

The large church on the left is the **Carmelite Church** and priory. Villegaignon Street opens on to **Bastion Square**; to your right, tucked inside the northern wall, the **Fontanella tea garden** is one of few eating places in Mdina and certainly the most spectacularly situated. The tea and cakes are good, too.

RABAT

For most visitors, Rabat exists as an add-on to Mdina – a place to visit only for its catacombs. Yet it exudes character in its confined streets of shops and town houses and deserves more attention. It is looked on as the suburb of Mdina; before the Arabs reduced Mdina's size the roles were reversed. Rabat's development has been accompanied by commercial growth and today it prospers alongside, rather than because of, Mdina.

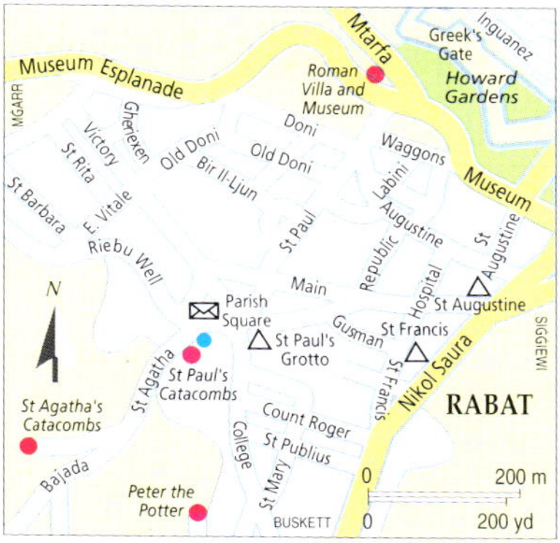

The Catacombs ★★★

Rabat has a vast network of catacombs and two in St Agatha Street are open to visitors. The most extensive, **St Paul's Catacombs**, are a labyrinth of tunnels, niches and rock tombs said to date from the 4th and 5th centuries. **St Agatha's Catacombs** are below the church dedicated to the saint, who fled to Malta from Catania in AD249 to escape persecution and is believed to have hidden in the underground cemetery before returning to Sicily to die a martyr.

As their belief that the dead should be buried conflicted with Roman law stipulating cremation, Malta's Christians adopted the burial method of the Palestinian Jews by carving these vast labyrinths. Family graves are cut into the rock walls; there are also stone canopies, benches and early communion tables used by the early Christians. Just visible on some tombs are the remains of frescoes.

Pope's Visit

On his 1990 visit to Malta, Pope John Paul II held prayers in the grotto beneath St Paul's church in Rabat. On a plaque outside the church on College Street is his parting 'God Bless Malta' prayer said at the airport. The yellow and white colours of the Vatican fluttered from every flagpole throughout the islands during his visit; many of these flags are still unfurled on special festive occasions.

St Paul's Church and Grotto ★★

On Rabat's Parish Square, site of Malta's first Christian community, the 16th-century, cross-shaped parish **Church of St Paul** ranks among the country's most impressive edifices – a product of the new prosperity

Left: *St Paul's Catacombs, largest of Rabat's ancient burial complexes.*
Opposite: *Ornate design high above Villegaignon Street in Mdina.*

THE MNARJA RACES

Rabat plays a big part in the festival on 29 June of St Peter and St Paul – the Mnarja (it derives from the Latin word *illuminaria*, to light up). The bareback horse and donkey races on the steep Saqqajja hill leading into Rabat from Valletta have been held since the time of the Knights. Winners are handed banners called *palji* from a loggia at the winning post; they are used as altar cloths for the following year. The feast of Mnarja also comes alive in Buskett Gardens, where crowds gather for a day of high revelry.

generated by the Knights. Though it dates from 1575, the church was largely rebuilt in the late 17th century and bears the hallmark of Lorenzo Gafa. The main altarpiece is by Mattia Preti.

Beneath the church is the **Grotto of St Paul**; according to tradition the Apostle lived and preached or was imprisoned in it during his winter in Malta. The cave's walls reputedly have the power of healing and it is said that no matter how much stone is scraped away by those seeking a cure, the cave's size never alters. The grotto contains a marble statue of St Paul, sculpted by Michelangelo's assistant Bernini and brought from Rhodes by Grand Master Manuel Pinto de Fonseca. In the early 1600s the cave was home to a Spanish nobleman, Giovanni Beneguas, who arrived to join the Knights but instead chose to live as a hermit and used his wealth to build the adjacent **Church of St Publius**. Across College Street in Wignacourt College is the small **St Paul's Museum**, with a miscellany of early finds.

St Augustine's Church, with its Renaissance-style façade, which is situated just off the town centre, was built by Gerolamo Cassar in 1571 and was his first church of major significance, preceding his Co-Cathedral in Valletta by just two years.

Below: *An outstanding example of mosaic work in the Roman Villa and Museum at Rabat. A Roman town flourished in the vicinity.*

Roman Villa and Museum ★★

At the far end of Howard Gardens, by the Greeks' Gate leading into Mdina, a small neo-Classical museum encloses the mosaic floor of a Roman villa and displays other Roman antiquities. The remains of the villa, among Malta's most significant Roman legacies and probably the home of a wealthy merchant, were discovered in 1881.

Mdina and Rabat at a Glance

Best Times to Visit

Mdina is best visited out of the peak holiday months of July and August, when there are fewer holiday-makers in its narrow streets and alleyways. At any time of year, go early or late in the day to avoid the crowds. Take in Rabat in **late June** if you can, when the Mnarja horse and donkey races are held as part of the festival of St Peter and St Paul.

Getting There

Mdina and Rabat sit in the centre of the island, within easy reach of Valletta, Sliema and St Paul's Bay. **Road** access is good from all parts of the island. **Bus** services to Mdina and Rabat include: **65** from Sliema; **80**, **81** from Valletta; **83** from Xemxija; **84** from Mtarfa; **86** from Buġibba.

Getting Around

Car use in Mdina is restricted to residents; the large car park outside the main gateway into the walled city usually has empty places and you can park all day for a few cents. Mdina is no place for cars anyway, as streets in the tiny city are narrow and usually packed with pedestrians. Horse-drawn *karrozzini* are allowed, however, and will give you a guided tour of both Mdina and neighbouring Rabat. Parking places are usually available down the hill facing St Paul's Church.

Where to Stay

The one hotel in the immediate area is the **Grand Hotel Verdala**, Inguanez Street, tel: 451700, fax: 451708. A four-star deluxe hotel which enjoyed its heyday in the 1970s, it is now being restored to its former glory.

Where to Eat

Eating places in Mdina tend to cater for those requiring either a full four-course blow-out or just tea and cakes – there's not much of a choice in between. Rabat is even shorter on restaurants, but the **Cosmana Navarra** offers snacks in the pleasant courtyard found opposite St Paul's Church.

Bacchus, Inguanez Street, Mdina, tel: 454981. Former munitions magazine and wine cellar within Mdina's fortifications offering a wide menu in the upper price range.

Medina, Holy Cross Street, Mdina, tel: 454004. Sophisticated dining in the Silent City.

Palazzo Costanzo, Villegaignon Street, Mdina, tel: 454625, 459384. Extensive Maltese selection and choice of good value tourist menus.

Fontanella, Bastion Street, Mdina. Light meals atop the bastions; tea and cakes are a speciality.

Ciapetti, St Agatha's Esplanade, Mdina. Tea gardens with views from the bastions; salads and snacks.

Tours and Excursions

Full-day and half-day **coach tours** are operated from Sliema and Buġibba to Mdina and Rabat. Time is allowed for a guided walk through the streets of the Silent City that includes a visit to the cathedral and Cathedral Museum; also a walk along the ramparts that offers splendid views across the island. Most tours also take in St Paul's and St Agatha'a Catacombs, Grotto of St Paul and Roman Villa and Museum in Rabat.

Two principal operators featuring tours of Mdina and Rabat are: Josephine's, 80 The Strand, Sliema, tel: 310435; and Nova Travel Services, Bay Square, Buġibba, tel: 575240, 575960.

Attractions presenting Mdina's colourful history are the **Mdina Dungeons** in St Publius Square, tel: 450267; the **Mdina Experience** in Mesquita Square, tel: 454322; **Medieval Times** in the Palazzo Notabile, tel: 454625; **Tales of the Silent City** in Villegaignon Street, tel: 451179; and **Knights of Malta** in Magazine Street, tel: 451342.

Useful Contacts

Tourist information, 1 City Gate, Valletta, tel: 237747.

Police, tel: 191 (general inquiries 224992).

St Luke's Hospital, tel: 234101, 241251, 247860.

7
The Centre

The central part of Malta, dotted with small towns and villages and crisscrossed by narrow country lanes, is defined by the Victoria Lines escarpment to the west, the concentrated urbanization of Valletta's various satellite towns and suburbs to the east and the Dingli Cliffs to the south.

The unmissable highlight in a tour of the centre is medieval **Mdina** (*see* p. 79). Beside the Victoria Lines are **Mosta** and **Naxxar**, and grouped in the geographical centre of the island is the prime residential area of the **Three Villages** – Attard, Lija and Balzan – with green San Anton Gardens between them. Nearer Valletta are the lively **commercial** centres of Birkirkara and Ħamrun; to the south of the **urban** area Qormi, Żebbuġ and Siġġiewi; and way out towards the southern cliffs the village of **Dingli**, with the green oasis of Buskett Gardens in the lee of Verdala Palace.

Don't Miss

*** **Mosta Dome:** its sheer size will not fail to impress.
** **Ta' Qali Craft Centre:** great for gifts and souvenirs.
** **Buskett Gardens:** some welcome greenery close to Verdala Palace.
** **San Anton:** attractive formal gardens by the President's palace.

Mosta **

The buzzing little town of Mosta is best known for the **Church of St Mary**, usually called simply either the **Mosta Dome** or the **Rotunda**, and visible from a large part of the island. At 37m (122ft) across, it is Europe's third largest unsupported dome, built between 1833 and 1860 in the style of the Pantheon and surpassed in size only by St Peter's in Rome and St Sophia's in Istanbul. Taller, but slightly narrower is the modern St John's Church at Xewkija in Gozo (*see* p. 117).

Opposite: *Mosta is dominated by its church; its mighty dome can be seen across the island.*

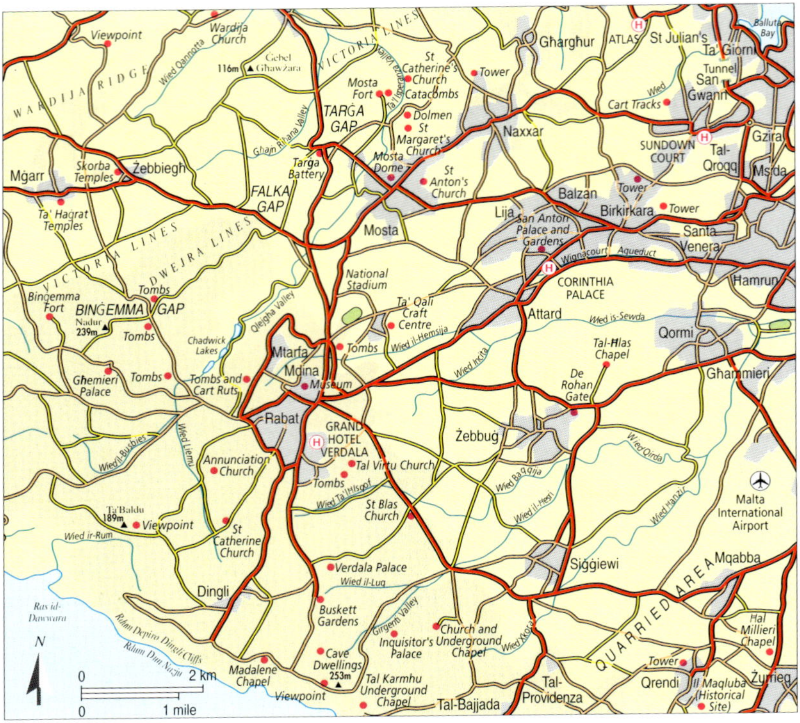

> **MALTESE BREAD**
>
> Malta's excellent crusty bread has its origins with the bakeries established by the Knights. Their recipes exist today with few modifications – the flat *ftira* bread is still popular while larger loaves have a thick crust and nutty flavour. **Qormi** is reputed to produce the best bread and at one time was known as the village of the bakers; in some towns and villages you can buy bread still hot from a wood-burning oven.

The Rotunda was built by volunteer labour, completed without the use of scaffolding and financed entirely by the local parish. On display is the casting of the World War II bomb that fell through the roof and rolled across the floor during a service but miraculously failed to explode. Just west of Mosta is the **Chapel of Tal L'Isperanza**, typical of the tiny wayside chapels found in more remote parts of the Maltese countryside.

Naxxar *

A neighbour of Mosta, Naxxar hosts Malta's annual International Fair in early July. It is one of the island's oldest parishes, dating from the mid-1400s; the parish church of **Our Lady of Victories**, completed in 1616, was

Tomasso Dingli's work, though the façade and side aisles were 20th-century additions. Dingli also designed the **Church of St Bartholomew** in Għargħur.

Watchtowers commanding the heights towards the Victoria Lines include **Gauci's Tower** in adjoining San Pawl Tat-Tarġa (meaning St Paul's steps), where it is believed the Apostle preached.

Above: *The Classical frontage of the Mosta Rotunda.*

Ta' Qali **

Situated on the former World War II airfield, **Ta' Qali Craft Centre** is Malta's largest local craft market. Craftsmen can be seen at work and their silver filigree jewellery, the famous coloured Mdina glassware, ceramics, wicker furniture, wrought ironwork and items of Malta stone are all produced on site and well displayed. Prices here are generally lower than in seaside souvenir shops.

Nearby rises the modern **Ta' Qali Stadium**, home of Malta's national soccer team and venue for the programme of matches in the island's Premier League. Beyond the small open-air theatre is the **Dinosaurs Exhibition**, with its life-size reproductions given the full sound and light treatment; here too is the **Malta Aviation Museum**.

The Three Villages *

The villages of Lija, Balzan and Attard contain many of the island's most desirable residences, some of which go back to the 17th century. **Lija's** reputation for having the best festa is well founded. It takes place around 8 August each year and is centred on the parish church of St Saviour. The church, with some fine frescoes, was completed in 1694 to designs by Giovanni Barbara and is widely regarded as his best work – he was only 24 at the time. Lija's Old Parish Church, built in the 16th century, is in St Saviour's Street; between them is the little Church of St Peter, dating from 1728.

In **Balzan's** main square, the Baroque parish Church of the Annunciation, from the late 17th century, has a decidedly Spanish appearance. On Three Churches Street are the small Church of St Roque, built in 1723 and dedicated to the protector of plague victims; the 15th-century Little Church of the Annunciation; and a small former church now in private hands.

Above: *A blaze of colour in San Anton Gardens, known for their variety of unusual trees and plants.*

Like Lija, **Attard** has a parish church designed by a man in his twenties – Tomasso Dingli was just 22 when he completed the Church of St Mary in 1616. Malta's finest Renaissance building, it has an excellent carved façade based on a Roman temple front.

The Three Villages are grouped around the lush greenery of **San Anton Gardens**, next to the Presidential Palace. The gardens, planned in the 17th century, provide a shady retreat in summer and contain some unusual species. There is also a small zoo.

The Central Towns

Birkirkara *

Often called B'kara, this is the largest of the towns and villages contributing to the urban and industrial sprawl west of Valletta. It is a typically Maltese working town, still showing its village origins in a centre dating from the 16th century.

The shining glory of Birkirkara is its tall Baroque parish **Church of St Helena**, designed by Maltese architect Domenico Cachia and built between 1735 and 1745. Cachia fashioned St Helena at the age of 27 and was later responsible for the brilliant rebuilding of the Auberge de Castile et Leon in Valletta. St Helena's external features include two attractive bell towers; the interior is richly gilded and carved, with excellent frescoes.

The **Church of the Annunciation**, the former parish church, had fallen into serious disrepair by the 1970s but is now restored. It was built in 1617 by Vittorio Cassar, son of better-known architect Gerolamo Cassar.

San Anton Palace

The grand house close to Attard of which the San Anton Gardens form part is now the official residence of Malta's President. It was built in 1625 as the country retreat of Grand Master **Antoine de Paul**, who found Verdala Palace too far from Valletta for his liking and is said to have upset the Inquisitor by staging a lavish banquet on his first night there. Formerly the Governor's residence, the palace is not open to the public.

Ħamrun *

The old town of Ħamrun, with its long main street of tiny shops, sits astride the Rabat road 2km (1¼ miles) from Valletta. Its small chapel of **St Mary of Porto Salvo** dates from 1736. In nearby **Santa Venera** is the country villa of **Casa Leoni,** with its outstanding formal gardens built in 1730 for Grand Master Manoel de Vilhena.

Qormi *

Once called Casal Fornaro (village of the bakers), Qormi has a long tradition for producing Malta's delicious crusty bread (*see* p. 90), though the old ways of baking are gradually giving way to more modern methods. Some fine buildings line its old streets, such as the **Stagno Palace** of 1589 in Dun Marigo Street and the parish **Church of St George**, which has an elegant Renaissance façade.

Żebbuġ *

Between Qormi and Żebbuġ, standing alone in the fields, is the small **Tal-Ħlas Chapel**, designed by Lorenzo Gafa in 1690. The entrance into Żebbuġ is through the **De Rohan Gate**, built in 1677 and a century later named after French Grand Master Emanuel de Rohan-Polduc. Inside the small town, which at one time had a reputation for producing sailcloth, are some fine houses of the 17th and 18th centuries and several interesting churches. Most imposing is the parish **Church of St Philip**, built in 1599 with similarities to St John's Co-Cathedral in Valletta; others are the **Chapel of St Roque** from 1593, the 18th-century **Our Lady of Angels** and the **Chapel of Tal-l'Abbundunata** from 1758.

The Glassblowers

Malta's coloured glassware makes one of the best-value and most distinctive souvenirs of the islands – and you can see it in the making. At **Mdina Glass**, on the edge of Ta' Qali Craft Centre, a giant shed houses the furnaces where craftsmen skilfully turn the molten glass into vases, bottles, ornaments and paperweights. The items come in an assortment of colours, but predominantly the attractive blue-green for which Mdina Glass is famous. There are bargains to be picked up on the seconds counter. Another manufacturer is **Phoenician**, on Manoel Island – it operates a free shuttle boat from the Strand at Sliema.

Siġġiewi *

The village of Siġġiewi is dominated by its splendid parish **Church of St Nicholas**, the inspiration of Lorenzo Gafa and built in 1675. It is widely held to be Malta's finest Baroque church and boasts one of the highest domes on the island.

Dingli *

Dingli, Malta's highest village with houses clustered round its silver-domed church, is best known for its cliffs. The

Below: *Towering Dingli Cliffs on Malta's scenic southern shore.*

CLAPHAM JUNCTION

Named after the busiest railway intersection in Great Britain, Clapham Junction on Malta is a major confluence of prehistoric 'cart ruts' near Buskett Gardens. Mysterious parallel grooves in the rock surface, they are believed to have been part of an early transportation system. Whether the ruts were carved by animal-hauled sledge or wheeled vehicle, or whether they were deliberately cut remains open to conjecture. What is surprising is that some lead straight over the cliff edge. You will need to look hard to locate them. There are similar cart ruts elsewhere in Malta and at Sannat in Gozo.

small village is 1km (⅔ mile) from the dramatic Dingli Cliffs that tumble down 253m (820ft) through cultivated terraces to the blue Mediterranean below. Some 5km (3 miles) offshore is the islet of **Filfla** (*see* p. 73).

The clifftops make fine walking country. Near the highest point is the **Madalene Chapel**, possibly the most isolated building in the Maltese islands and open only on 22 July, the Feast of St Magdalene. A wall plaque informs those seeking sanctuary from the law that they will not find it there – a warning dating from the early 17th century, when the Knights sought to restrict the protection afforded by the church.

Verdala Palace ★★

Overlooking the lush greenery of Buskett Gardens, Verdala Palace was built in 1586 as a luxurious summer retreat for extrovert French cardinal Grand Master **Hugues Loubenx de Verdalle**. It was designed by **Gerolamo Cassar** as a fortified castle and today, as the official summer residence of the President, it is used to host visiting VIPs. A flight of steps crosses the moat from which was cut the palace's building stone; inside a superb elliptical staircase in one corner leads to the first floor. The great hall contains frescoes of Verdalle's life, while in the first-floor dining room is the chess board chiselled out of the stone floor by French prisoners in 1812.

Below: *Verdala Palace overlooks the verdant Buskett Gardens, with their plantations of firs, cypress, oaks and citrus trees.*

Buskett Gardens ★★

This delightfully green area, last vestige of the forest that once covered Malta, is popular for its flora in spring and its wooded shade in summer. The name stems from the Italian *boschetto* (little wood). In late June big crowds gather here for the **Mnarja** festival.

The Centre at a Glance

Best Times to Visit

The centre of Malta is best enjoyed in **late spring**, when you can appreciate the island's rural aspects and admire the wild flowers, especially in the fields below Mdina's citadel and on the high Dingli cliffs. If you are there in summer, the thick tree coverage of Buskett Gardens provides shady relief from the powerful sun.

Getting There

Malta's central area is within easy reach by **road** of Malta's main centre of Valletta and Sliema, the St Paul's Bay resort district and the hotels of the north. The **bus** connections to the south include: **40** Valletta–Balzan–Lija–Attard; **43**, **44**, **45**, **47**, **49**, **50**, **52**, **53**, **57** Valletta–Birkirkara–Balzan–Mosta; **54**, **56** Valletta–Balzan–Naxxar; **55** Valletta–Naxxar–Għargħur; **65** Sliema–Mosta–Ta' Qali–Rabat; **74** Valletta–San Anton–Attard; **81** Valletta–Rabat–Buskett–Dingl; **88** Valletta–Qormi–Żebbuġ; **89**, **90**, **91** Valletta–Qormi.

Getting Around

A comprehensive **road** network links the towns and villages of Malta's central area. Though road signage has improved in recent years, it may be difficult finding directions if you stray from the main roads outside the built-up areas on to the network of lanes crisscrossing the countryside. There is no road access to the sea on Malta's southern coast west of Għar Lapsi; the road that runs along the top of Dingli cliffs affords some fine views out to sea towards the islet of Filfla. **Bus** services, linking towns and villages in the area with Valletta, offer good connections within the region.

Where to Stay

Malta's central region has only two hotels – the Grand Hotel Verdala at Rabat (*see* p. 87) and the Corinthia Palace. There are no holiday apartments or guesthouses in the area. Plenty of hotel and self-catering accommodation can be found by the coast in the Sliema/St Julian's area and in the St Paul's Bay resorts.

Corinthia Palace, tel: 440301/9, fax: 465713. Five-star elegance in one of Malta's few inland hotels, situated by San Anton Gardens. Opened by the Duke of Edinburgh in 1968, it now contains a health spa.

Where to Eat

There aren't too many places to go if you get hungry in middle Malta. The Corinthia Palace Hotel and a small selection of eating places in Mdina (*see* p. 87) are the best bet, plus one beyond Dingli with good sea views. Do-it-yourself picknickers should try Qormi, the village of the bakers, for a crusty loaf, perhaps with local goat's cheese and washed down with a bottle of Maltese wine.

Bobbyland, Panoramic Road, Dingli, tel: 452895. Reasonably priced Maltese specialities at this eatery on Dingli cliffs.

Tours and Excursions

Half-day and full-day **coach tours** operate from Malta's principal resort areas to attractions in the centre of the island. Among sites visited are the Ta' Qali Craft Centre, where time is allowed for shopping and visiting the Dinosaurs Exhibition, and Mosta Dome. Tours to the region also visit the green areas of San Anton Gardens and Buskett Gardens. Two of the leading operators with tours that take in the centre of the island are Josephine's, 80 The Strand, Sliema, tel: 310435; and Nova Travel Services, Bay Square, Buġibba, tel: 575240, 575960. A five-hour **Vintage Village excursion** to Naxxar includes a tour of the village by 1920s-style bus operated by Captain Morgan Cruises, tel: 343373, 331961 or 336981.

Useful Contacts

Tourist information, 1 City Gate, Valletta, tel: 237747.

Police, tel: 191 (general inquiries 224992).

St Luke's Hospital, tel: 234101, 241251, 247860.

8
The North

Malta's northern region, though often remote and detached from the rest of the island by the Victoria Lines escarpment, has developed as a significant tourist area around **St Paul's Bay**, named after the Apostle's well-chronicled shipwreck of AD60. The twin resorts of **Buġibba** and **Qawra** link hands across the Qawra peninsula that separates St Paul's Bay and Salina Bay – Buġibba full of holiday apartments and Qawra with some large hotels. Beyond Buġibba is the original fishing village of St Paul's Bay, now enmeshed in the coastal development that extends onwards past **Xemxija Bay**, the innermost reach of St Paul's Bay, and up the steep hill to overlook the Mistra Valley.

The bays and inlets of the north contain almost all of Malta's sandy beaches – from the wide expanse of Mellieħa Bay to the sand of aptly named Golden Bay on the opposite coast and other stretches of beach beyond the Marfa Ridge.

Don't Miss

** **Popeye Village:** tumble-down Sweethaven brought back to life at Anchor Bay.
** **Victoria Lines:** renovated century-old defences built by the British.
** **Għajn Tuffieħa Bay:** arguably the prettiest of Malta's sandy bays.
** **San Pawl il Baħar:** the little fishing village of St Paul's Bay.

St Paul's Bay

The generous sweep of St Paul's Bay is Malta's second holiday area after Sliema and St Julian's. It tends to include Qawra, although most of that town is around the headland facing Salina Bay.

The coast road hugging Malta's barren northern shore from Baħar iċ-Ċagħaq to **Salina Bay** leads past the modernized Coastline Hotel of the 1960s and then the long-disused but still pungent **salt pans** cut by the

Opposite: *Excursion boats alongside St Paul's Bay jetty at Buġibba. Trips take in the bays of northern Malta and Comino.*

St Paul's Shipwreck

In the Bible, Chapter 27 of The Acts of the Apostles tells of the ship carrying St Paul and St Luke to Rome for trial running aground 'where two seas met'. It continues: *'The forepart stuck fast, and remained unmoveable, but the hinder part was broken with the violence of the waves. . .and so it came to pass, that they escaped all safe to land. And when they were escaped, then they knew that the island was called Melita'.*

Knights. Just off the road is the **Kennedy Grove** memorial to the assassinated US President, now sadly unkempt and in need of attention. The Maltese, with the best of intentions, erect monuments to the fallen and worthy but then tend to forget about them and frequently allow them to fall into a state of disrepair.

Qawra *

To the north lies Qawra which, before the building of the Qawra Palace and Suncrest hotels in the mid-1980s gave it a shot in the arm, was a quiet resort of scattered aparthotels and holiday apartments. Behind the seafront apartments development is still proceeding, though at a slower pace – lessons appear to have been learned from the sporadic and haphazard growth of Buġibba.

Above: *St Paul's Bay is one of several fishing harbours dotted about Malta.*

Buġibba ★

The souvenir shops start immediately past the New Dolmen Hotel. This is Buġibba, despised by locals for its un-Maltese appearance but a place that welcomes many thousands of low-budget holiday-makers each year. Throughout the 1980s Buġibba resembled a building site as developers, having sought to cash in on the tourism boom of the late 1970s, ran out of money. Now most of the work has been completed, though the end result is hardly beautiful and the whole sadly lacks planning. Alongside such long-standing enterprises as the Tartan Bar and Bognor Regis, a large seafront café, there is a rash of fast-food outlets, bars and mini-markets that testify to the resort's popularity.

San Pawl Il Baħar ★★

After the brash, the beautiful. The old fishing harbour of St Paul's Bay, with its brightly painted *luzzu* craft and neat little church, is a treat after featureless Buġibba. The **Church of St Paul**, open only in summer, was given its distinctive arcade in the 17th century and bears panels of New Testament quotations in several languages relating to St Paul's time in Malta. Dominating the little harbour, but not too intrusive, is the Gillieru Harbour Hotel, opened in 1994.

The restored **Wignacourt Tower**, built by Grand Master Alof de Wignacourt in 1610, overlooks the harbour. Across the bay beyond Xemxija is the coastal indentation of **Mistra Bay**, where a former abandoned farmhouse, reputedly a haunt of smugglers, has been converted into a restaurant.

ST PAUL IN MALTA

St Paul and his fellow prisoners were welcomed ashore after their shipwreck. The **Church of St Paul** in San Pawl Il Baħar is said to be on the site where St Paul shook off a deadly viper into the fire and won over the islanders. The spring of **Għajn Razul**, or **Apostle's Fountain**, is supposedly where St Paul struck a rock to provide drinking water for the survivors. St Paul spent three months in Malta, preaching the Gospel (he converted the Roman governor Publius to Christianity) and healing the sick before continuing his journey via Syracuse to Rome.

Mellieħa Bay **

This is Malta's largest beach, 600m (⅓ mile) long and resplendent with bright umbrellas in summer, when it throngs with local families and tourists. Dinghies, pedaloes and windsurfers are available for water sports fans; there are a couple of no-frills beach cafés serving chips with everything and a regular supply of Malta's excellent soft ice cream.

Across the road that curves round the bay are the wetlands of the **Għadira Nature Reserve**, which offers some measure of protection to birdlife from Malta's destructive hunters. The merciless killing by the Maltese of what little wildlife their country possesses has received scant attention from successive governments, fearful of forfeiting precious votes should they attempt to curb this unsavoury national pastime.

UNDERWATER SAFARIS

If you fancy exploring the deep without getting your hair wet, the Underwater Safari boat of the **Captain Morgan** company operates several cruises daily from the small quay at Buġibba. A sophisticated improvement on the glass-bottomed boat, the Underwater Safari craft accommodates passengers in a glass-sided lounge below deck that affords excellent views of marine life through the crystal clear water.

On the far side of the bay is the Mellieħa Bay Hotel, which enjoys one of the most striking seascapes on the island across the water to **Mellieħa** village, crowned by its parish **Church of Our Lady of Victory** high on the ridge. Down the hill a short way, a long flight of steps leads to the chapel of **Our Lady of the Grotto**, carved from the rock with a faded fresco of the Virgin Mary attributed to St Luke.

Mellieħa, balanced about its steeply sloping main street of shops and restaurants, is a bustling community of distinctive character. A self-styled rural hub, it has origins in the 15th century and was one of Malta's earliest parishes. Until the early 1990s, the village was regularly jam-packed with cars; now the bypass road with its breathtaking coastal panorama whisks traffic bound for Mellieħa Bay and Gozo well away from the built-up area.

From Mellieħa there is a fine vista of the rocky island of Comino, with Gozo's church-dominated skyline beyond. On the slopes around Mellieħa the grapes are grown for the islands' limited production of red and white wine.

Marfa Ridge **

The high ground beyond Mellieħa Bay belongs to the Marfa Ridge, protected by the 1649 **Red Tower** of the Knights. Driving along the narrow ridge road past the Red Tower to **Ras il-Qammieħ** there are stunning views across the Comino Channel to Gozo and Comino.

From a shrine at the crest of the hill, the narrow, pot-holed road on the right follows the ridge to the **Madonna statue** and a tiny **chapel** on a remote and windy part of the island favoured by the hunting fraternity.

All the side lanes from the ridge road head down across the rugged landscape to little bays beyond the ridge. These include **Ramla Bay**, **Armier Bay** with its blue-and-green-painted holiday homes and the attractive yet oddly named **Slug Bay**, situated below the **White Tower**. These bays attract many more Maltese than tourists, who tend to favour bigger stretches like Mellieħa Bay and Golden Bay. In winter, the extreme north of the island is deserted, its holiday homes barred and bolted – as such, it makes fine walking country.

A few hundred metres before reaching the Gozo ferry terminal of Ċirkewwa, a side road leads uphill to a small cliff-top car park overlooking **Paradise Bay**.

Popeye Village

Whether or not you saw the 1980 film *Popeye*, the film set at **Anchor Bay** is a real treat. The 17 painted wooden water's-edge houses of tumble-down Sweethaven have been revived after threatening for years to collapse into the sea through neglect. The Paramount film by Robert Altman starred Robin Williams as Popeye and Shelley Duvall as Olive Oyl and is available on video. A cinema by the entrance shows a film about the making of Sweethaven. A horse-riding trail from stables near Golden Bay passes by Anchor Bay.

Opposite: *The Knights' Red Tower fortification.*
Below: *Painted wooden houses at Popeye village.*

Northwest Malta

Overlooking **Golden Bay** are the huge Golden Sands Hotel and, by the edge of the sands, a smaller building dating from the 1950s that was Malta's first beach-side hotel. Around the flat-topped headland is **Għajn Tuffieħa Bay** (the name means 'eye of the apple'), prettier even than Golden Bay and reached by a long flight of steps starting from beside the long-redundant Riviera

MALTA'S TOURISTS

Malta's tourist arrivals have increased steadily since a slump in the mid-1980s, from 745,943 in 1987 to 1.2 million in 1999 – more than three times the islands' population. Though July and August are traditionally the peak holiday months, with around 150,000 visitors apiece, Malta welcomes more off-season arrivals now than ever. The **British**, with around 450,000 annually, make up 38% of Malta's visitors; the **Germans**, with 195,000, represent 17%. Some 65,000 cruise passengers call each year. Malta is popular with elderly tourists, many of whom spend the whole of winter on the island.

Martinique Hotel, now in a state of partial collapse. Both beaches can be reached by bus from Valletta and become crowded in summer, Golden Bay especially so.

Generally quieter is the smaller **Ġnejna Bay** (it translates as 'small garden'), with a neat line of boathouses cut into the limestone cliff. The bay is signposted west of Mġarr through the green Ġnejna Valley, abundant with figs, vines and tall bamboo. **Mġarr** itself (like Żebbuġ and Rabat it has a twin of the same name in Gozo) has the large **Church of the Assumption**, which was funded by villagers through the sale of eggs – and in recognition the dome was given the appearance of an egg.

Historic Sites

Northern Malta has some of the island's oldest archaeological remains – earlier even than the Ġgantija temples on Gozo. The **Skorba** site, just outside the village of Żebbieħ, provided Malta with its earliest Neolithic ruins; evidence of two temples and several houses indicate this was a village of some size. Another prehistoric site on the edge of Mġarr is **Ta' Ħaġrat**, with what is left of two temples of the Skorba type believed to date from 3000–2500BC. Just outside the village stands a modern mansion, **Zammitello Palace**. Guarding the coastline are the **Għajn Znuber** watchtower at the western end of the Marfa Ridge, a tower between Golden and Għajn Tuffieħa bays and the **Lippia Tower** inland of Ġnejna Bay.

While it is known that Malta prospered under the Romans, little evidence of the period remains. Some villas have been excavated and in 1929 the **Roman baths** near Għajn Tuffieħa came to light. The site was restored with UNESCO money in the 1960s.

Below: *The golden sand of Għajn Tuffieħa Bay, one of Malta's prettiest beaches.*

The North at a Glance

Best Times to Visit

Summer is the most popular season for visiting Malta's north, with the beaches attracting thousands of visitors between June and September. Prospective winter vacationers should consider staying in Sliema or St Julian's, where there is much more going on out of season.

Getting There

The north of Malta is best reached at the end of a scenic drive along the **coast road** from the Sliema/Valletta direction. Fine views of Gozo and Comino unfold the further north you go, along with some excellent panoramas of the rugged northwest coast.

Getting Around

There are fewer roads in Malta's northern reaches owing to the rugged nature of the landscape. The main **road** from St Paul's Bay passes Mellieħa Bay before climbing Marfa Ridge and dropping to the Gozo ferry point at Ċirkewwa.

Bus services, most linking the resorts and bays of the north with Valletta, also offer good connections around the region.

Where to Stay

Qawra/St Paul's Bay

Suncrest, Qawra Coast Road, tel: 577101, fax: 575478. Big and brash, it dominates Qawra's seafront with its water-side lido. At the very top of the four-star band.

Qawra Palace, Qawra Coast Road, tel: 580131, fax: 580662. Good sea-facing location for the Suncrest's four-star neighbour; attractive seafront lido.

New Dolmen, Qawra, tel: 581510/8, fax: 581532. Large modern four-star built around Neolithic remains at the meeting of Buġibba and Qawra.

Corinthia Mistra Village Clubhotel, Xemxija Hill, tel: 580481, fax: 582941. Best holiday complex in the islands, with apartments set neatly around two pool areas.

Mellieħa area

Mercure Grand Selmun Palace, Selmun, tel: 521040, fax: 521159. Hilltop location for this four-star popular with continental visitors.

Mellieħa Bay, tel: 573841, fax: 576399. Four-star favoured by the British, with splendid views across the bay and beach to Mellieħa village.

Bays to the north

New Paradise Bay, tel: 573981, fax: 573115. Large white-walled four-star next to Gozo ferry terminal, Ċirkewwa.

Golden Sands, tel: 573961, fax: 580875. Large and popular three-star next to Golden Bay's sandy beach.

Ramla Bay, tel: 522181, fax: 575391. Remote north coast four-star at the end of a lane off Marfa Ridge facing Comino.

Where to Eat

Savini, Qawra Road, tel: 576927. Magnificent, rural, upper range Italian cuisine with excellent service.

Da Rosi, Church Street, St Paul's Bay, tel: 571411. Fish restaurant, all-round menu.

Gillieru, St Paul's Bay seafront, tel: 573480, 573269. Inexpensive with good reputation for fish.

Palazzo Santa Rosa, Mistra Bay, tel: 582736. Slightly more expensive, in converted farmhouse by the sea. Excellent range of starters.

It-Tokk, Suncrest Hotel, Qawra, tel: 577101, fax: 575478. Traditional Maltese dishes served buffet-style in a rustic setting.

Coral Reef, Suncrest Hotel, tel: 577101, fax: 575478. Moderate prices with good fish selection.

The Arches, Main Street, Mellieħa, tel: 573436, 520533. More expensive, but with reputation for top-class cuisine.

Tours and Excursions

Captain Morgan Cruises, tel: 343373, 331961, operates **boat trips** from Buġibba to Comino and around Gozo; they also operate an **Underwater Safari boat**.

Maltaqua, tel: 571873, 572558, offers diving tuition, ranging from beginners to advanced level.

Useful Contacts

Tourist information, Triq l-Alka, Buġibba, tel: 576079.

9
Gozo

Most visitors to Gozo are day-trippers, arriving by ferry in mid-morning and leaving in late afternoon. The little island welcomes 400,000 day visitors annually and local businesses thrive as a result. But to fully appreciate Gozo you need to stay for a bit longer, enjoy the relaxed lifestyle of this traditional farming and fishing community, and recognize the world of difference that exists between the island and its larger neighbour.

Gozo is just over a quarter the size of Malta – 15km (9½ miles) long by 7km (4½ miles) at its widest point – while its rocky shoreline of bays and inlets measures 43km (27 miles). Of the Maltese islands' total population of 350,000, some 26,000 live in Gozo. While Malta's people seem ever to be on the move, however, those in Gozo give the impression of having discovered the ultimate laid-back approach to life.

This is where the Maltese go when they want to get away from it all. Gozo is different enough to feel like another country, yet it is only a 20-minute ferry trip away. And though many Gozitans 'emigrate' to Malta, they remain first and foremost proudly Gozitans, faithful to the isle they call Għawdex (pronounced Ow-desh). This was an Arabic corruption of earlier names and has always been preferred by the locals to the Spanish version, Gozo, which was imposed upon them.

Thanks to its distinctive blue-clay soil, Gozo stays green even in high summer, when its neat, cultivated terraces contrast with Malta's sun-baked surfaces.

Don't Miss

*** **Victoria's Citadel:** visit the cathedral and take in Gozo from the ramparts.
*** **Ġgantija temples:** impressive legacy of a flourishing ancient culture.
** **Xlendi:** still a gem of a village, though seriously under threat from overbuilding.
** **San Blas Bay:** Gozo's tiniest bay, well worth the long descent.
** **Country walks:** enjoy the clifftop rambles for which Gozo is renowned.
* **Sunset at Dwejra:** see the sun hit the horizon near Gozo's most westerly point.

Opposite: *Rural Gozo looking from the Citadel.*

Year of Revenge

Gozo's blackest year was 1551, when **Dragut Rias** led a Turkish raid to exact revenge for the death of his brother, who seven years previously had been captured and killed on Gozo. The Turks invaded the island, killing or carrying off into slavery almost the entire population of 5000. Fourteen years later, Dragut himself perished during the Great Siege of Malta.

The Gozitans have long been farmers and part-time fishermen – today the smaller island provides Malta with much of its produce, hand-tilled in tiny fields and often transported by donkey cart. Villages crown the hilltops, both as a measure of defence and to leave the valley floors free for crops; in spring the countryside bursts forth in a profusion of wild flowers.

The proximity of the two islands means that Gozo's history and culture have been inextricably linked to those of Malta, though both were self-governing from the Roman period until the arrival of the Knights. In modern times, Gozo has again established some autonomy, albeit limited. The island was given its own government ministry in 1987 and it has achieved a good deal. Compared to its larger neighbour, the roads are better, the capital and villages are cleaner and tidier and there is generally a stronger environmental awareness.

The Maltese government is trying to establish Gozo as an upmarket holiday spot and is encouraging the development of top-quality hotels such as L'Imġarr. The government is aware, however, that over-development could easily destroy Gozo's appeal and is now restricting the building of new holiday accommodation to deluxe standard. In keeping with this upmarket image are converted farmhouses and modern apartments with their own swimming pools.

Right: *Country transport: the donkey cart is still widely used in Gozo's rural areas.*

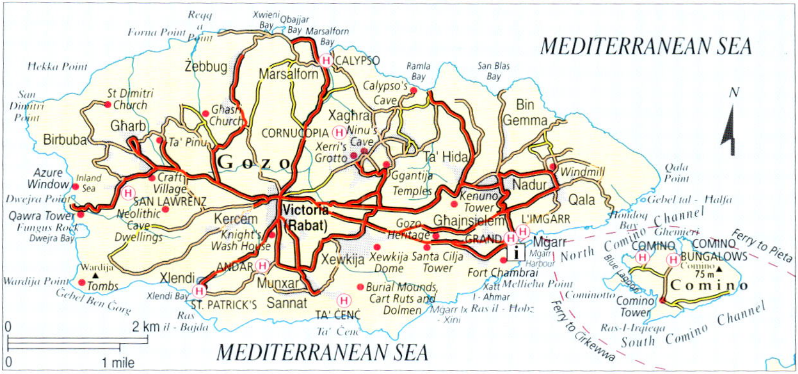

Victoria

Gozo's chief town and traditional capital begs comparison with Mdina – a hilltop citadel rising proudly above the landscape, its sheer curtain walls visible from afar. Within the ramparts, a maze of alleyways disorientates the visitor; at the foot of the walls a wider mesh of side streets makes up Gozo's social and commercial hub. The city, formerly **Rabat**, was renamed Victoria in 1897 to celebrate Queen Victoria's diamond jubilee – a move not welcomed by the locals, who still refer to Rabat (meaning 'suburb') rather than Victoria, which can cause some confusion with the Rabat in Malta.

All the island's main roads radiate from the capital and you will need a good map to find your way around the island on the minor roads. However, Victoria is a place to visit rather than to stay in, as there are no hotels and few restaurants.

The Citadel ***

Gozo suffered severely at the hands of the Turks and other marauding raiders throughout the Middle Ages and the only solution appeared to be the construction of a city stronghold in which the population could gather in times of danger. The mighty bastions you see today, built around 1600 and funded jointly by King Philip II of Spain and the Gozitans themselves, were never put to

Gozo Heritage

Gozo's 7000-year history is recalled in Gozo Heritage, a series of tableaux housed in a typical Gozitian farmhouse on the Victoria road just outside the village of Għajnsielem (open daily 10:00–17:00). Animated life-size figures in period costume recall historical scenes, from the legend of Calypso via the culture of the Phoenicians, Romans, Arabs, Normans, early Christians and the Knights. Gozo's part in the Great Siege of 1565 is recounted, as are the influences of Napoleon and Nelson. Its role in World War II is also portrayed.

Above: *The cathedral and remains of medieval houses within the Citadel, whose walls were built nearly 400 years ago as a refuge against the Turks.*

the test. By that time the Turks had fled back east, leaving the Gozitans in relative peace – though spasmodic raids occurred into the 18th century.

In 1637 a law requiring all islanders to sleep within the Citadel was rescinded; the people moved out and thus began the decline of the old city's importance. Many of the vacated buildings within those walls were destroyed by the 1693 earthquake. Today the towering ramparts embrace the cathedral, a number of museums, some craft shops and the crumbled medieval dwellings that are now the subject of a restoration programme. Don't leave the Citadel without walking round the ramparts – the 360-degree panorama that unfolds offers the best views of Gozo.

Into the Breach

Having stood firm for more than 300 years, the Citadel's curtain walls were finally breached in 1956 – not by an act of war but by workmen providing a grander entrance and exit for the feast day procession of Santa Maria on 15 August. Much criticized at the time, the new opening nevertheless created a grander view of the cathedral and the apron of steps leading up to it. The former main gateway is at the end of the approach road to the right of the breach.

The Cathedral **

From the outside it lacks the ornamentation of other prominent Maltese churches; on the inside the creation of Maltese architect **Lorenzo Gafa** is far from plain. The cathedral was started in 1697, replacing a previous church on the site, and completed in 1711. Once inside look skywards for the interior's focal point, the beautifully proportioned painting of the 1730s by Italian artist **Antonio Manuele** – a *trompe l'oeil* which gives the illusion of a vast dome. The cathedral roof is actually flat, funds having run short before its completion.

The Museums ★★

Victoria's Citadel, a historical treasure in itself, includes several small museums dedicated to Gozo. The **Archaeological Museum** in the 17th-century Palazzo Bondi, former home of an endowed Gozo family, contains excavated relics of the Ġgantija temples and includes a stone phallic symbol; there is also a model of the temple site, along with Roman amphorae (wine jars) and other finds.

In the vestry behind the cathedral, the **Cathedral Museum** has a collection of vestments, ceremonial pieces, manuscripts and portraits. There is also a ceremonial landau from around 1860 used by the Bishop of Gozo. The **Folklore Museum** recounts Gozo life down the years in displays occupying three medieval houses; crafts are shown here and also in the **Crafts Centre**, where products are displayed but are not for sale – business cards of the makers are alongside.

The **Natural Science Museum**, in a former storeroom of the Knights, identifies Gozo's flora and fauna and has a section on the marine environment. By the Citadel wall, the 17th-century **Knights' Armoury**, a former British barracks, is home to an array of weaponry that includes both lances and cannonballs.

Race Days in the City

Victoria's main thoroughfare, **Republic Street**, was once called Racecourse Street after the trotting races still held there on the feast days of St George in mid-July and Santa Maria (Feast of the Assumption) on 15 August. A huge crowd of Gozitans and many weekend visitors from Malta turn out for the festivities. Shops and houses line Republic Street, along with two small theatres which double as cinemas.

Below: *Stepped alleyway in Victoria's Citadel, part of a maze of passages within the fortified walls.*

The Main Square (It-Tokk) ★★

While the Citadel on its bluff first catches the eye, the real heart of Victoria is its main square, **Pjazza Independenza** – better known by its old name of **It-Tokk**, meaning 'meeting place'. The small, tree-lined square at the top of Republic Street is fringed with tiny shops and bars and has a daily morning market selling fruit, vegetables and local craftware. In the centre of the square is a statue of Christ that commemorates the fallen of World

Getting to Gozo

- **Ferries** of the Gozo Channel Company run between Ċirkewwa in Malta and Mġarr in Gozo and operate more or less hourly round the clock in summer and from early until late in winter. Crossing with a car is both efficient and inexpensive. The crossing takes approximately 20 minutes.
- Thankfully, Gozo is still spared the noise and environmental pollution of its own airport. For visitors seeking a faster alternative to the ferries, a small heliport near Xewkija handles the **helicopter** link with Malta International Airport.

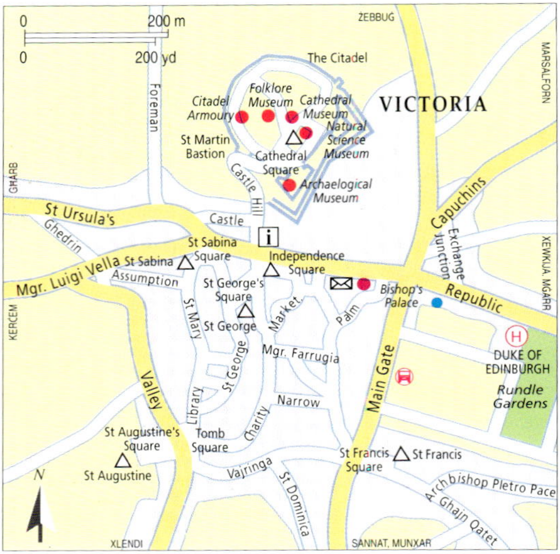

Below: *Xagħra's Ta-Kola windmill, a well-preserved example of the strong rural heritage of Gozo.*

War II; on the edge the newly renovated **Church of St James**, from 1740, and the semi-circular **Banca Giuratale** built by Grand Master Manoel de Vilhena in 1733 to house the council of Gozo. It is now the site of government offices.

St George's Basilica ★★

Behind It-Tokk, in the Pjazza San Gorg among the balconied streets of the old town, is the Baroque St George's Basilica, traditionally Gozo's first parish church. It was built in the 1670s and has been beautified over the years; fine artistic works inside include Mattia Preti's painting of St George with his foot victoriously placed on the head of the dragon. The bronze altar canopy is styled on one by Bernini in St Peter's in Rome.

Northern Gozo

Gozo's northern region is characterized by the green sweep of the long Marsalforn Valley, flanked by the two hilltop villages of Żebbuġ and Xagħra and ending in the attractive little seaside resort of Marsalforn. The bluff supporting Victoria's Citadel rises high above the head of the valley, which extends for some 3km (2 miles) towards the sea and is a picture of wild flowers in spring and early summer. There is a good road from Victoria to Marsalforn and also out to Żebbuġ and Xagħra; narrow lanes descend from the hilltop villages to the coast. A statue of Christ the Saviour stands atop a conical hill above the Marsalforn Valley.

Above: *Wild spring flowers bloom in the Marsalforn Valley.*

Xagħra *

Crowned by its mighty 19th-century **Church of Our Lady of Victories** fronting the wide village square, Xagħra (pronounced Shar-ra) dominates Gozo's northern landscape; the village is one of Gozo's few growth areas and could soon rival Victoria for size. Just off the square is the distinctive and well-restored **Ta-Kola windmill** of 1725, one of several that once dotted the island, and now a small rural museum. Also in Xagħra is the Edward Lear-inspired **Pomskizillious Toy Museum** at 10 Ġnien Xibla Street, which includes exhibits more than 160 years old.

Two limestone caves discovered below houses in the village – **Ninu's Cave** (in 1888) and the larger **Xerri's Grotto** (in 1923) – have fascinating examples of stalactites and stalagmites. The owners will lead you down and point out the unusual geological forms created over the millennia.

Calypso's Isle

Local legend – and the Greek scholar Callimachus in the 3rd century BC – holds that Gozo is **Ogygia**, isle of the sea goddess Calypso in Homer's *Odyssey*. Calypso is said to have lured the Greek hero Odysseus on to the island as he returned from Troy and held him captive for seven years in the cave high above Ramla Bay before being ordered by Zeus to release him. The view across the golden beach of Ramla Bay is more impressive than Calypso's Cave, which despite its alluring name is just a narrow opening at the top of the rocky cliff.

Gozo's Farmhouses

If you want luxurious accommodation off the beaten track, Gozo has the answer in its converted farmhouses. No expense has been spared in upgrading these rustic rural dwellings into superb and spacious holiday villas, often with their own swimming pool, courtyard and often a walled garden and rooftop terrace. This is upmarket tourism – you may even find a jacuzzi in your little corner of Gozo.

Above: *The ancient structures at Ġgantija, most impressive of Malta and Gozo's temple sites.*

Ġgantija Temples ***

The largest and best preserved of the islands' prehistoric temple sites, Ġgantija is claimed to be the world's oldest free-standing structure – older even than the Egyptian pyramids and Stonehenge in Britain. According to legend, the massive blocks of Ġgantija (the word means 'gigantic') were carried from Ta' Ċenċ in the south of the island by a female giant between 3600 and 3000BC – some are as much as 6m (20ft) high and weigh many tonnes.

The complex, on a fenced-in hilltop site a few minutes' walk from the centre of Xagħra, was unearthed in 1827 and comprises two temples, built several centuries apart, with a forecourt. Each temple has five lobe-shaped apses leading off a central corridor; features within are the floor libation holes, limestone blocks with spiral decoration, an oracle hole and a stone recess for washing feet. The large altar blocks were almost certainly used for the sacrifice of animals.

Nearby is the **Brochtorff Circle** underground cave complex with stone walls and arches that Gozo's inhabitants used for burials between 4000 and 2500BC. The site, excavated since 1987, has yielded some fine figurines and skeletal remains.

Marsalforn **

Long a quiet fishing village, today Marsalforn is Gozo's chief holiday resort. It is still small and the setting attractive, with bars and restaurants aplenty around the bay and an array of souvenir shops well stocked with home-knitted woollens for which Gozo has earned its high reputation.

The whole seafront area has been recently redesigned, with better paving along the promenade and the short sand and shingle beach improved. A short distance to the

west, at the foot of the narrow road from Żebbuġ, are the bays of **Xwieni** and **Qbajjar**, both good for swimming. From **Żebbuġ** itself, which is stretched out along the top of the ridge north of Victoria, there are superb views towards Marsalforn and west across the Għasri Valley, where a little sea inlet offers some good bathing.

Ramla Bay **

This is Gozo's one real sandy beach, with sand as golden as you will find anywhere and the water inviting, though care must be exercised because of currents. The beach is generally less crowded than those in Malta, even on the hottest days. This was a favoured landing place for invaders in the Middle Ages, prompting the Knights to construct an underwater defensive wall across the bay's entrance, the remains of which can still be seen. To the west, near the top of the cliff, is the legendary **Calypso's Cave**; inland among the dunes is the site of a **Roman villa**.

Above: *Gozo's chief resort, Marsalforn, was once a small fishing village.*
Left: *The Knights' salt pans at Qbajjar.*

The Salt Pans

Around the headland west of Marsalforn, at **Qbajjar**, the salt pans date back 250 years to the latter days of the Knights and are still very much in use. Locals harvest the white salt crust left by evaporated seawater in the rectangular rock-cut chambers, gathering several tonnes each year.

Festa Fireworks

The annual village festas culminate in some memorable firework displays as the strong rivalry between parishes means that each is determined to put on bigger and better exhibitions than their neighbours. In the days preceeding the festa, petards explode in ever-increasing numbers above the village in a countdown to the big weekend – if you are in Malta in July or August you will be well aware of them. Highlight is the *giggifogu*, where fireworks mounted on poles in the village square are set off one at a time in a truly spectacular show.

Above: *The limestone Azure Window near Dwejra Point.*
Below: *Dwejra's cliffs aglow at sunset.*
Opposite: *The national shrine of Ta' Pinu Basilica.*

Western Gozo

The barren landscape that falls away from San Lawrenz towards the sea near Gozo's westernmost point has a fascination bred by the feeling that you might just have reached the ends of the earth. This bleached coastline of cliffs and caves strikes a pleasing contrast with the deep blue Mediterranean and erosion has created a fine natural arch, the **Azure Window** or *Tieqa Zerqa*. Tread lightly across this bridge of fossilized seashells – its collapse has been predicted for years.

A short way offshore in Dwejra Bay is the sheer-sided **Fungus Rock** (also *Il-Ġebla tal-Ġeneral* or General's Rock), whose unusual vegetation cover was highly prized by the Knights as a cure for dysentery and haemorrhaging. The only access was by rope and pulley from the Qawra Tower on the shore; anyone found attempting to steal the red 'fungus' was put to death.

The third feature of geological interest is the **Inland Sea**, a sheltered seawater pool flanked by high cliffs and linked by a natural passageway to the open sea. Small boats leave here for trips through the tunnel and along the coast; a little rustic bar among the boathouses provides welcome refreshment.

Gozo Lace

The ladies of Gozo have a well-earned reputation as being among the world's best lacemakers. The craft was introduced from Genoa in 1846 in an effort to raise the standard of living of the poorest islanders and developed into a fully fledged industry, supporting tourism and providing Gozo with its best-known souvenirs. The lace, called *bacilli*, is made to a stencilled design on a lacemaker's pillow by using bobbins; the finished articles – tablecloths, handkerchiefs, mats, table napkins, doilies and bookmarks – are extremely good value.

Ta' Pinu Basilica **

Alone in the fields between Għarb and Għammar stands Malta's national shrine of Ta' Pinu, a Romanesque centre of pilgrimage that was given basilica status in 1932. Passing a small 16th-century chapel here in 1883, local spinster Carmel Grima heard a voice telling her to pray; a friend, Francesco Portelli, affirmed that he had also heard the voice. They prayed together for his sick mother, who made an unexpected recovery.

Miracle cures followed in the area and from thanksgiving offerings the present sanctuary was built in the 1920s; it incorporates the original chapel, whose early caretaker Pinu Gauci lent his name to the site.

The Villages

Of Gozo's smaller villages, **Għarb** is among the prettiest. Its ornate and balconied houses cluster around the 17th-century Baroque Parish Church of the Immaculate Conception with its unusual concave façade and sculptures of Faith, Hope and Charity. The **Għarb Folklore Museum**, in an 18th-century village house, highlights Maltese and Gozitan traditions.

Within a kilometre of Għarb are the hamlets of **Birbuba**, **Għammar** and **Santa Pietru**. At the top of the road leading downwards to Dwejra Point is **San Lawrenz**; to the right of the road which heads back towards Victoria is the **Ta' Dbiegi Craft Village**, where you can see lacemaking and weaving and watch pottery, ceramics and glass being made. It is open year round.

The Nuns' Steps

To the right of the bay as you face the sea at Xlendi, there is a flight of steps cut into the rock. Climb them for an excellent view of Xlendi's tiny waterfront and then descend to **Caroline's Cave**, a small natural cove named after a wealthy spinster who in 1889 founded a group of nursing nuns, the Dominican Sisters of Malta. She paid for these steps to be cut so the nuns could enjoy private bathing – the gate the sisters locked behind them remains today.

Southern Gozo

The wild cliffs of southern Gozo are the highest on the island, rising nearly 150m (500ft) either side of Xlendi Bay. The compact resort of Xlendi sits at the seaward end of a 3km (2 mile) valley leading southwest from Victoria; halfway down, a side road heads eastwards across the valley to Munxar. Occupying two hills either side of the Hanzira Valley beyond Munxar are the villages of Xewkija and Sannat.

Xlendi **

The scenic road to Xlendi descends quickly from Victoria and runs down a steep-sided valley with views across to Munxar. On the way it passes the 17th-century **Knights' Wash House** in Victoria's 'suburb' village of Fontana, built by the order over a spring that supplied the locals with water.

A delightful little seaside village, Xlendi has maintained its appeal as Gozo's second resort to Marsalforn despite living in the shadow of a massive bank of tourist apartments. On the tiny promenade, a handful of open-air cafés and knitwear shops vie for business either side of the St Patrick's Hotel. In summer, small boats bob in front of the narrow sandy beach, sheltered by tall cliffs and guarded by the Xlendi Tower, one of many such defences ringing the Maltese islands and built in 1658.

Below: *Tiny Xlendi at the head of its landlocked bay. The calm water in the bay is ideal for swimming.*

Above left: *Ideal for relaxation: the cafés along the promenade at Xlendi.*
Above right: *Lacemaking on Gozo, the island's most famous home industry.*

Sannat *

The small village of Sannat is known for its lacemaking and for one of the really outstanding hotels in the Maltese islands, Ta' Ċenċ. The hotel, which blends inconspicuously with its extensive grounds, takes its name from the cliffs to the south, the highest on Gozo and nesting site for a variety of bird life. Near the hotel, ancient burial mounds, a dolmen and cart ruts of the kind found on Malta (*see* p. 94) are evidence that the area was occupied in prehistoric times. Sannat's **Parish Church of St Margaret** was built in 1718 on the site formerly occupied by a smaller church.

Between Sannat and Xewkija, a narrow lane leads down through the steep-sided Ħanzira Valley to the attractive narrow inlet of **Mġarr ix-Xini**, a quiet spot which is good for bathing. The short walk from Ta' Ċenċ leads across open countryside, with excellent views to the west of the sheer cliffs so closely identified with this part of the island.

Xewkija *

Dominating the skyline of the area, and indeed that of the whole of Gozo, is Xewkija's mighty **Rotunda**, or dome, the fourth largest in Europe and only just beaten into third place by the Mosta Dome on Malta.

Xewkija's Rotunda

The church in Xewkija which incorporates the famous Rotunda is dedicated to St John the Baptist. It was financed by parishioners and built by local labour between 1952 and 1971 on the site of a small 17th-century Baroque church. A measure of its vast size is that Xewkija's entire population of more than 3000 would only make for a medium-sized congregation. The Rotunda has been compared in style and proportion to Santa Maria della Salute in Venice.

Above: *The harbour of Mġarr, entry port to Gozo. Above the harbour is Fort Chambrai, built in the 18th century by the Knights.*

No Fat Cats Here!

Don't feel pity for the thin cats you see on your travels in Malta. All Maltese cats are naturally slimline and are equipped to cope with the hot summer weather – they are not necessarily in need of a good meal. Many live wild and enjoy very different lives to their north European cousins, with hand-outs from benevolent hoteliers and fishermen taking the place of canned cat food. Whole families of cats can be seen living together in relative harmony. Note also the long pointed face characteristic of the Maltese cat.

Eastern Gozo

Mġarr **

Although Mġarr is the main port of entry from Malta, many visitors pass straight through towards Victoria and then the resorts of Marsalforn and Xlendi. In fact Eastern Gozo is the most peaceful and rural part of the island and Mġarr itself remains a favourite subject of Maltese watercolour artists. The view from the ferry is of a busy little harbour packed with *luzzu* boats, yachts and ferries, and a skyline pierced by the spires of two churches. The graceful 19th-century Gothic-style **Our Lady of Lourdes** is nowadays dwarfed by the much larger church of Għajnsielem, the neighbouring village on the road to Victoria.

High to the left are the ramparts of **Fort Chambrai**, ambitiously planned as a fortress town in the early 1700s by Grand Master Manoel de Vilhena but never completed as such. The fortifications of the Knights' last major defensive work were eventually finished thanks to the private funding of the Order's French admiral Jacques François de Chambray. When the French invaded in 1798 it was the only fortification to put up any resistance; later it served as a British garrison, a place of convalescence for

Allies wounded at Gallipoli in 1915, a mental hospital, a low-grade tourist complex and as government housing. The latest of many plans call for it to be turned into a high-class, 250-bed holiday village. On the opposite side of the harbour, offering guests exceptional views across the Comino Channel to Comino and Malta, is Gozo's second five-star hotel, the **L'Imġarr**.

Nadur *

On a hill north of Mġarr, 150m (500ft) above sea level, is the large and prosperous village of Nadur – in Arabic the name means 'summit' – from where vigilant locals kept watch for unwanted visitors in the time of the Knights. The splendid **Parish Church of St Peter and St Paul** was designed in the 18th century by Maltese architect Giuseppe Bonici and contains some fine stained glass.

On the edge of nearby Qala is a distinctive Gozo windmill of the 19th century, which was in use until the 1980s. The small village also has the 17th-century **Sanctuary of the Immaculate Conception**, on the site of an 11th-century chapel, and the square-towered **Church of Santa Marija** with its neat churchyard overlooking the sea.

Beyond Nadur and Qala there are the small but exquisite beaches of San Blas and Hondoq bays.

San Blas Bay

- One of the most scenically attractive little beaches of the Maltese islands is at **San Blas Bay**. Follow the sign to the bay out of Nadur and take the single-track road downwards – above the bay there is parking space for three cars at a squeeze. A surfaced footpath leads steeply down past cultivated terraces to the tiny sandy bay. It is one of the truly peaceful spots on the planet.
- Another small beach at the eastern end of the island is at **Hondoq Bay**. The road east from Qala winds down to the usually deserted sandy inlet, where the water takes on a brilliant turquoise appearance to rival that of Comino's famed Blue Lagoon.

Below: *San Blas Bay, one of Gozo's best-kept secrets.*

Safe Haven

Comino takes its name from an aromatic cumin plant once found here. Now the island is more noted for its rocky landforms, with its barren cliffs a home for large numbers of seabirds. While Comino's bird population multiplies during the migration season, no bird is endemic to the island. There is a surprisingly varied wildlife that includes bats, rabbits and hedgehogs; hardy trees include olives, carobs, acacias and pines.

Below: *The Comino Tower, guarding the channel between Malta and Gozo.*

Comino

In mid-channel between Malta and Gozo sits the island of Comino, all 2.5 km^2 (1 sq mile) of it, which can be reached from both Malta and Gozo. Historically a pirates' haven, Comino is today the refuge of tourists seeking solitude, relaxation and every water sport under the furnace-like summer sun. There are no cars or roads on Comino; a short coastal path links the island's low-rise four-star tourist accommodation, the Comino Hotel and Comino Bungalows, in adjacent bays.

From the Gozo ferry you can make out the sparkling turquoise waters of the **Blue Lagoon** on the fractured coast between Comino and the islet of Cominotto. From mid-morning to early afternoon it usually has a full complement of tourist boats and it is a favourite haunt of scuba divers, who have plenty to explore in a fascinating underwater world of caves and grottos.

The island's dominant feature is the **Comino Tower**, built in 1618 by Grand Master Alof de Wignacourt to protect the Comino Channel from raiders and later used as a hunting lodge. There are also the remains of a former isolation hospital used by the British in World War I, the small Gothic **St Mary's Chapel** dating from the late 1600s in which masses are still held, possibly the world's smallest police station and a pig farm. Five people live on the island year-round.

Gozo at a Glance

Best Times to Visit

Malta's sister islands of Gozo and Comino are best enjoyed in **springtime**, when visitors can enjoy their fine rural aspects and admire Gozo's profusion of wild flowers.

Getting There

The Gozo Channel Company operates a year-round **car ferry** service; Malta Air Charter operates a **helicopter** service from Malta International Airport. (*See* Travel Tips on p. 125 for details.)

Getting Around

Finding your way around Gozo is easy, as nearly all roads radiate from the capital Victoria. **Car hire** is available in Gozo from Victor Borg Enterprises, tel: 552908, 551866. It is wise not to rely too heavily on public transport; **buses** tend to be operated by the villages and at times to suit the locals. Service **25** runs with some regularity between the Mġarr ferry point and Victoria, but after that finding a bus can be difficult. **Taxis** are available, but at a cost. A **motor launch** operated by the Comino Hotel runs in summer from Mġarr to Comino.

Where to Stay

Northern Gozo
Cornucopia, 10 Ġnien Imrik Street, tel: 552633, fax: 552910. Superb four-star farmhouse conversion at Xagħra with great pool area.
Calypso, Marsalforn Bay, tel: 562000, fax: 562012. No-frills three-star hotel on the quayside.

Southern Gozo
Ta' Ċenċ, tel: 556819, fax: 558199. Outstanding five-star hotel with bungalow-style rooms in extensive grounds near Sannat.
St Patrick's, 12 Xlendi Seafront, tel: 562951, fax: 556598. Comfortable four-star hotel at water's edge.

Eastern Gozo
L'Imġarr, tel: 560455/7, fax: 557589. Five-star clifftop hotel above Mġarr harbour with spectacular views of Comino and Malta.

Comino
Comino, tel: 529821/9, fax: 529826. Hotel and bungalows in adjacent bays provide the only accommodation on tiny Comino.

Where to Eat

Cornucopia Hotel, Gnien Imrik Street, Xagħra, tel: 556486, fax: 552910. Great lunchtime pasta, good evening selection.
Vineyard, Mġarr Road, Victoria, tel: 559976. Large medium-priced menu in newly renovated surroundings.
Jeffreys, Għarb Road, Għarb, tel: 561006. Splendid value, hand-written menu which changes daily; rural ambience. Closed in winter.
Kenur, Victoria Road, Xlendi, tel: 551583. Serves a good mid-priced selection. Also has a fixed-price menu.
Oleander, Victory Square, Xagħra, tel: 557230. Great value, authentic Gozitan meals served overlooking the square.
St Patrick's, Xlendi Seafront, tel: 562951. Good à la carte menu at reasonable prices by the sea.

Tours and Excursions

Full-day **excursions** operate to Gozo from the resorts on Malta. **Jeep safaris** go off the beaten track to see parts of the island not seen on regular coach tours. **Evening trips** to Gozo take in the sunset at Dwejra. The principal operators are Josephine's, tel: 310435; and Nova Travel Services, tel: 575240, 575960. **Boat trips** from Sliema and Buġibba visit Comino: Captain Morgan, tel: 343373, is the chief operator. **Dive specialists** offering tuition include: Calypso Diving Centre, tel: 562000; Frankie's Gozo Diving Centre, tel: 551315; St Andrew's Divers Cove, tel: 551301.

Useful Contacts

Tourist Information, Victoria, tel: 558106, 564104; Mġarr Harbour, tel: 553343.
Gozo Heritage, tel: 551475.
Police, tel: 562040.
Craig Hospital, Victoria, tel: 556851.

Travel Tips

Tourist Information

There are Malta National Tourist Offices abroad in France (Paris), Germany (Frankfurt), Holland (Amsterdam), Italy (Milan), the United Kingdom (London) and the USA (New York).

Malta Tourism Authority, newly embracing the National Tourism Organization, Hotel and Catering Establishments Board and Institute for Tourism Studies, is at 280 Republic Street, Valletta CMR 02, tel: 224444/5, 225048/9, fax: 220401.

Tourist Information Offices within Malta can be found at Malta International Airport, tel: 69996073/4; 1 City Gate, Valletta, tel: 237747; Triq l-Alka, Buġibba, tel: 576079; 1 Palm Street, Victoria, Gozo, tel: 558106, 564104; and Mġarr Harbour, Gozo, tel: 553343.

Entry Requirements

Nationals of most countries, including the United Kingdom, may enter Malta for up to three months on production of a valid passport. A visa is required in a few cases. Non-Maltese travellers must complete an embarkation or disembarkation card before passport control, whether on arrival or departure.

Customs

Duty-free allowances are 200 cigarettes (or 50 cigars or 250g of tobacco), one litre bottle of spirits and one litre bottle of wine, and a reasonable amount of perfumes and toilet water per adult visitor. Gifts to residents are subject to VAT. There are duty-free shops in the arrival and departure halls at Malta International Airport; also at the Sea Passenger Terminal.

Health Requirements

No health precautions are needed by visitors to Malta. Smallpox and cholera vaccination certificates are required by arrivals from infected areas and yellow fever immunization by travellers arriving within six days of leaving an infected area.

Getting to Malta

By air: The national airline Air Malta operates direct scheduled services to Malta International Airport from some 45 points throughout Europe, the Middle East and North Africa. Malta is also served by airlines of many other European countries, including Alitalia, Lufthansa and Swissair. It is also possible to book seats on charter flights operating to Malta – contact your travel agent. Flight inquiries within Malta, tel: 249600.

By sea: The high-speed catamaran services of Virtu Ferries, tel: 318854, operate from Pozzallo, Catania and Syracuse in Sicily to Malta. The Gozo Channel Company, tel: 556114, operates the inter-island service between Malta and Gozo.

What to Pack

In summer the minimum is required – lightweight casual clothing which can be easily washed suffices and you don't need to take pullovers, cardigans or jackets as it stays warm until late evening. If you burn easily, take something to cover the shoulders and arms as Malta's sun can be intense. Children should wear a teeshirt over their swimwear in the pool or sea to prevent burning. If you feel like glamming up in the evening, you won't feel out of place as the Maltese tend to dress up rather than down when they go out. In winter, although temperatures might look good, warm clothing is necessary as the air can be damper than expected and the stone buildings can be cold.

Money Matters

Currency: When the Maltese decided to dispense with the pound as a unit of currency – it was seen as a relic of British rule – the way was clear to introduce a fresh name for its money. However, it opted for the lira (Lm), which can cause confusion with the Italian lira. To complicate matters further, some shops still use the £ sign and most shopkeepers refer to Malta pounds rather than liri (the plural of lira).

There are 100 cents to the lira. Notes are Lm 2, Lm 5, Lm 10 and Lm 20; coins are Lm 1 and 1, 2, 5, 10, 25 and 50 cents.

Exchange: Malta's two main banks are the Bank of Valletta and Mid-Med Bank; both have branches throughout the island with currency exchange facilities. There is a 24-hour exchange facility at Malta International Airport. Other banks are Lombard Bank and APS Bank. Smaller bureaux de change are found in Valletta and tourist areas.

The maximum sum in local currency allowed into the country is Lm 50 per person; the limit on departure is Lm 25 per person.To change Maltese currency back it is necessary to present exchange receipts.

Bank **opening hours** show seasonal variation. Summer (15 June–30 Sept): 08:00–12:00 Monday to Friday, 14:30–16:00 Tuesday and Friday, 08:00–11:30 Saturday; winter (1 Oct–14 June): 08:30–12:45 Monday to Friday, 16:30–18:00 Tuesday and Friday, 08:30–12:00 Saturday. Some branches are open for longer hours than these.

Foreign exchange facilities are also selectively available in summer from 16:00–19:00 and in winter from 15:00–18:00.

Credit cards: International credit cards are widely accepted in hotels, restaurants and most shops. Expect to use cash in smaller shops, bars and snack-bars.

Tipping: Taxi drivers 10%; restaurants 10%, unless a service charge has been added to the bill; porters 15c to 20c per piece of luggage.

Taxes: VAT at 10–15% was reintroduced in Malta from 1998. Prices displayed include VAT; the law states that a receipt must be given and retained by the customer for at least 24 hours.

USEFUL PHRASES

ENGLISH	MALTI
How much?	*kemm?*
How far?	*kemm bogħod?*
Good morning	*bonġornu*
Good evening	*bonasira*
Good night	*il-lejl it-tajjeb*
Goodbye	*saħħa*
How are you?	*kif int?*
To the left	*lejn ix-xellug*
To the right	*lejn il-lemin*
Thanks...	*grazzi*
...very much	*grazzi ħafna*
Excuse me	*skużani*
I beg your pardon.	*skużi*
Please	*jekk jogħġbok*
Sorry	*jiddispjaċini*
For sale	*għal bejgħ*
Too dear	*għoli wisq*
Very cheap	*irħis ħafna*
One	*wieħed*
Two	*tnejn*
Three	*tlieta*
Four	*erbgħa*
Five	*ħamsa*
Six	*sitta*
Seven	*sebgħa*
Eight	*tminja*
Nine	*disgħa*
Ten	*għaxra*
Eleven	*ħdax*
Twelve	*tnax*
Twenty	*għoxrin*
One hundred	*mija*

Accommodation

Malta has hotels and self-catering properties to suit every pocket, from deluxe hotels to no-frills guesthouses, and luxury villas or converted farmhouses to basic apartments. Hotels are graded from one to five stars and tourist villages and guesthouses from first to third class. Aparthotels, offering apartment-style accommodation with full hotel facilities, range from first to fourth class. There are no official camping or caravan sites in the islands.

Eating Out

This is simply no problem. Eat cheaply or expensively according to your pocket, your mood and your taste – from a simple bowl of pasta in the sun to something far more formal with several courses that demands collar and tie. Malta's resort areas of Sliema, St Paul's Bay and St Julian's have a high concentration of places to eat out and other restaurants are scattered throughout the islands. For the widest choice of restaurants head for the St Julian's/Paceville area – here there are also a large number of discos and music bars that will appeal to younger visitors. The capital Valletta has few restaurants; a much wider choice is available in nearby Sliema. Options include Indian, Chinese, Greek, Italian, Turkish and Russian, besides traditional Maltese, pizzerias and pasta-houses aplenty. You can also dine well in hotel restaurants, many of which serve a traditional Sunday lunch.

Transport

Though substantial investment in Malta's road system in recent years has improved internal communications, journey times are generally slow and the Valletta–Sliema–St Julian's conurbation, Ħamrun and Birkirkara can be especially busy. The underground multi-storey car park for 1800 cars outside Valletta's City Gate is handy for the capital as parking within Valletta is severely restricted by the narrowness of the roads.

While road signposting has been improved, you will probably still find yourself navigating by the sun in remoter country areas where signs are occasional or non-existent. In Gozo this is less of a problem – most roads radiate from the island's capital Victoria.

Road: Car hire in Malta is among the cheapest in the Mediterranean; rates are fully inclusive and the daily rate usually works out cheaper if the car is hired for a week or longer. Even hiring a car at Malta Airport can pay for three days rental by saving a Lm 10 taxi fare each way.

All valid national driving licences and international driving licences are recognized. While Maltese law allows driving from 18 years with no upper age limit, some companies restrict car hire to those over 25 and under 70. International car rental companies such as Avis, Hertz, Budget and Europcar Interrent operate alongside local companies, of which Alpine and Wembleys are two of the largest. If you are involved in an accident, call the police; do not move the car before the police have made their on-the-spot report, or it may invalidate your insurance.

Road rules: Driving is on the left in Malta, a legacy of British rule; the speed limit is 40kph (25mph) in built-up areas and 64kph (40mph) elsewhere. Road signs are international; traffic lights have been installed throughout the island in the last few years. Petrol stations selling super grade and unleaded are open Monday–Saturday from 07:00–18:30 in summer; 07:00–18:00 in winter. A few garages open on a rota until midday on Sundays and public holidays.

Taxis: Travelling by taxi is not cheap and fares increase sharply after midnight. Taxis are white (usually Mercedes), with distinctive red number plates. They are metered to display government-controlled prices, though the meter is not always switched on – if this is the case, make sure you agree the fare in advance. Taxis are readily available at the airport and on ranks in the main resort areas; some

Conversion Chart

From	To	Multiply By
Millimetres	inches	0·0394
Metres	yards	1·0936
Metres	feet	3·281
Kilometres	miles	0·6214
Kilometres square	square miles	0.386
Hectares	acres	2·471
Litres	pints	1·760
Kilograms	pounds	2·205
Tonnes	tons	0·984

To convert Celsius to Fahrenheit: x 9 ÷ 5 + 32

larger hotels have their own rank. Note that Maltese taxis do not cruise the streets in the hope of picking up a fare. It is possible to hire a taxi for a day's sightseeing, but again agree the price first.

Buses: A ride on one of Malta's old yellow bone-shaker buses should not be missed. Public transport in Malta operates frequently and is amazingly cheap, with most fares between 11 and 15 cents (on certain routes between main resort areas the cost of a ride can be more). Routes radiate from the Valletta bus terminus outside City Gate to every town, village and sandy beach in the island. In Gozo, buses (grey with a red stripe) serve the main villages from Victoria but run only infrequently.

Ferry: A ferry service operates half-hourly in summer from the Strand in Sliema (the area is still referred to as the Ferries from the steam ferries of old) across Marsamxett Harbour to Valletta. It is a good alternative to the road trip – and quicker, too. Departure times are advertized at the Sliema departure point.

The **Gozo ferry** service is operated by The Gozo Channel Company. The 6km (4 mile) crossing from Ċirkewwa in northwest Malta to Mġarr in Gozo takes about 20 minutes. The car-carrying service operates more or less hourly in summer (every two hours at night); the frequency changes from late September to late June, when there are no night sailings. Winter crossings can be affected by weather conditions – if in doubt, check with the Gozo Channel Company, tel: 243964–6; in Gozo, tel: 556114, 561622. Return fares are Lm 5.75 for a car and driver, Lm 1.75 per adult and 50c per child, confusingly paid at a kiosk on the Gozo side before the return journey.

Helicopter: The 10-minute helicopter journey between Malta International Airport and Xewkija in Gozo is the quickest connection between the islands. Primarily intended for passengers arriving and departing through Malta International Airport and connecting to and from Gozo, the service easily allows for a day return trip to either island – there are up to 18 flights daily each way in summer. Advance reservation is recommended, tel: 662211–6 in Malta; 557905 or 561301 in Gozo; or see a travel agent. Malta Air Charter also operates helicopter sightseeing.

Public Holidays

Malta observes the following public holidays:

1 January • New Year's Day
10 February • St Paul's Shipwreck
19 March • St Joseph
31 March • Freedom Day
Good Friday (variable)
1 May • Workers' Day
7 June • 'Sette Giugno'
29 June • St Peter and St Paul
15 August • The Assumption
8 September • Our Lady of Victories
21 September • Independence Day
8 December • The Immaculate Conception
13 December • Republic Day
25 December •

Business hours

Offices: Offices in Malta and Gozo switch over to summer working hours for July, August and September – generally 07:30–13:30. For the rest of the year, working hours are 08:30–17:00 with a break for lunch.

Shops: Shops open from 09:00–13:00 and again from 16:00–19:00 on Monday–Saturday; they are closed on Sunday and public holidays (*see* panel). Many shops in tourist areas stay open throughout the day.

Time

Malta is on Central European Time, one hour ahead of Greenwich Mean (Universal Standard) Time in winter and two hours ahead of GMT from the last Sunday in March to the last Sunday in September. The islands are six hours ahead of the USA's Eastern Standard Winter Time and seven hours ahead in summer.

Communications

Big investment in Malta's telephone system has worked wonders in recent years, for making both international and local calls.

Most telephone numbers in Malta and Gozo are six-figure and there is no area code. To call Malta from abroad dial the international access code followed by 356. For local inquiries dial 190 and for overseas inquiries dial 194. Calls made from Gozo to Malta require the prefix 8.

The Telemalta Corporation provides a 24-hour phone and fax service from its St Julian's office; other phone/ fax offices around the island are in South Street, Valletta; Bisazza Street, Sliema; Qawra; St Paul's Bay; Malta International Airport (on the ground floor); and Victoria on Gozo.

STD dialling is available to most countries, including the UK (code 0044), USA and Canada (001), South Africa (0027) and Australia (0061). Phone cards valued from Lm 2–5 can be purchased from any Telemalta branch, post offices, Mid-Med banks and some newsagents.

There are **post offices** in most towns and villages; hours are usually 07:45–13:30 but can vary. The main post office in St Zachary Street, Valletta, is open until 18:00 on weekdays; Gozo's main post office is in Republic Street, Victoria. Stamps are also available from newsagents.

Electricity

The power supply is 240 volts, single phase, 50 cycles. Standard (UK) rectangular three-pin plugs are needed.

Weights and Measures

Malta uses the metric system for all measurements.

Health Services

There are two general hospitals in the islands: St Luke's at Gwardamanġa, near Valletta, tel: 234101, 241251, 247860; and Craig Hospital in Victoria, Gozo, tel: 556851. There are also health clinics in several towns and villages. Pharmacies are open Monday–Saturday from 08:30–13:00 and 15:00–19:00; on Sunday, one pharmacy per district opens in the morning on a roster listed in the newspapers (or call the Police HQ, tel: 224992).

Most hotels have the services of a doctor on call. In emergency, tel:196 in Malta or 556851 in Gozo. Malta has reciprocal health agreements with several countries, including the United Kingdom.

Health Precautions

Visitors to Malta need no inoculations, but should take care with the strong sun.

Emergencies

On Malta dial police 191 (general inquiries, tel: 224992), ambulance 196 and fire 199. On Gozo, dial police 562040, ambulance 556851 and fire 562040. There are police stations in most villages.

Good Reading

Gerada, Eric & Zuber, Chris. *Malta – An Island Republic*. Editions Delroisse.

Schermerhorn. *Malta of the Knights*. AMS Press, New York.

Bradford, Ernle. *The Great Siege – Malta 1565*. Penguin Books, London.

Attard, Joseph. *Britain and Malta – The Story of an Era*. Publishers Enterprises Group, Malta.

Bradford, Ernle. *Siege of Malta 1940/1943*. Penguin Books, London.

Blouet, Brian. *The Story of Malta*. Progress Press, Malta.

Monsarrat, Nicholas. *The Kappillan of Malta*. Pan, London.

Ross, Geoffrey Aquilina. *Images of Malta*. Miranda Publications, Malta.

Etiquette

As Malta is a strongly religious country, visitors to the islands' cathedrals and churches should dress accordingly. Men should ideally wear long trousers rather than shorts (though this is rarely, if ever, enforced); women should cover their shoulders (a wrap may be available at the church door) and avoid wearing shorts or mini-skirt. Topless bathing is against the law.

Language

While Malti is the national language, English is widely spoken and understood, particularly in the resorts.

INDEX